Rainbow Edition

Reading Mastery III
Textbook A

Siegfried Engelmann • Susan Hanner

Macmillan/McGraw–Hill

Columbus, Ohio

Portions of this publication have been adapted from DISTAR READING III, Student Materials. © 1972, 1973, Science Research Associates, Inc. All rights reserved.

SRA Macmillan/McGraw-Hill
250 Old Wilson Bridge Road
Suite 310
Worthington, Ohio 43085
Printed in the United States of America.
ISBN 0-02-686388-X
   3 4 5 6 7 8 9 0 RRC 99 98 97 96

Textbook A

Contents

LESSON A

A

1	2	3
six	fly	legs
insects	of	title
three	another	name
grass	butterfly	rule
	grasshopper	

Insects Ⓐ

*Here is a rule about insects: **The body of any insect has three parts.** Ⓑ

insect   spider

An ant is an insect. A fly is an insect. A butterfly is an insect. A grasshopper is an insect. Ⓒ

Is a spider an insect? No. A spider looks like an insect, but the body of a spider does not have three parts. Ⓓ A spider's body has two parts. So a spider is not an insect. Ⓔ

Here is another rule about insects: **All insects have six legs.** Ⓕ

An ant has six legs. A fly has six* legs. Spiders do not have six legs. Spiders have eight legs. Ⓖ ❀ 3 ERRORS ❀

LESSON B

A

1	2
water	living
babies	know
insect	need
people	spiders
grow	seeds
	butterfly

B

Living Things Ⓐ

Here is a rule about all living things: **All living things grow, and all living things need water.** Ⓑ

*Are trees living things? Yes. So you know that trees grow and trees need water.

Dogs are living things. So what do you know about dogs? Do dogs grow?Ⓒ Do dogs need water? Ⓓ

People are living things. Do people grow?Ⓔ Do people need water? Ⓕ

Here is another rule about all living things: **All living things make babies.** Ⓖ

Trees are living things. So trees make baby trees.

Are fish living things?Ⓗ So what do fish make? Ⓘ

Are spiders living things? Ⓙ So what do spiders make? Ⓚ

Remember the rule: All living things* make babies. Ⓛ ✿ 3 ERRORS ✿

LESSON C

A

1	2
start	fishing
grow	underline
over	deeper
could	living
water	ground
carry	

B

Trees Ⓐ

*Trees have roots. The roots are under the ground. Ⓑ The roots do two things. The roots hold the tree up to keep it from falling over. The roots also carry water from the ground to all parts of the tree.Ⓒ Trees could not live if they did not have roots.

PICTURE A

Here's another fact about trees. Trees do not grow in the winter because the ground is cold. **D** In the spring, trees start to grow. **E** The sun makes the ground warmer in the spring. First the top of the ground* gets warm. Then the deeper parts of the ground get warm. **F**

Small trees begin to grow before big trees grow. **G** Small trees grow first because their roots are not very deep in the ground. Their roots are in warmer ground. So their roots warm up before the roots of big trees warm up. **H** ❋ 3 ERRORS ❋

PICTURE B

LESSON D

A

1	2
today	listen
shirt	woman
rule	store
kind	striped
agree	brother
think	

B

Tim and His Brother Ⓐ

Tim and his brother had a room. The room had walls that were dirty. Tim's brother said, "Let's paint the walls today." Ⓑ

Tim told his brother, "I want white walls."

Tim's brother said, "I want red walls." Ⓒ

*The boys did not agree. Tim kept telling his brother, "Listen, I want white walls."

At last, Tim looked at his shirt. It had stripes. Tim said, "I've got it. Let's have striped walls. The walls could have red stripes and white stripes." Ⓓ

Tim's brother said, "I agree. Let's have striped walls." Ⓔ

So Tim and his brother went to the paint store. The woman in the store asked them, "What kind of paint do you want?"

Tim said, "We want striped paint."

Do you think the woman could mix paint* that was striped? Ⓕ ❋ 3 ERRORS ❋

LESSON 1

1	2	3
cross	mixed	swimming
cover	pull	opened
page	hair	other
canoe	think	first
	your	box
	ball	frog

4	5	6
field	boxes	himself
wear	finish	somebody
full	food	inside
grew	forest	
	tiger	

B

1. grapes   playing football   shirt

2. pants   cutting hair   frog

3. pets   field

4. canoe   fish   bell   fishing pole

5. log   tiger

1.

2.

3.

4.

5.

C **The Tiger and the Frog**Ⓐ

Tom's brother had two pets. One pet was a
frog. The other pet was a big mean tiger.Ⓑ
Tom's brother kept his pets in boxes. One day
Tom said, "I want to play with your pet frog."

Tom's brother said, "Here is the rule about where I keep that frog. **I keep the frog in the box that is striped.**"Ⓒ Then Tom's brother said, "Don't get mixed up because I keep my pet tiger in one of the other boxes."Ⓓ

Tom said the rule to himself. Then he went into the room with the boxes. Here is what Tom saw.Ⓔ 🌸 2 ERRORS 🌸

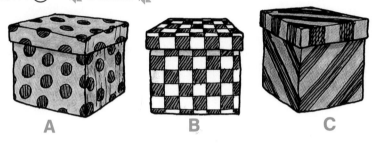

A   B   C

Tom looked at box A. He tried to think of the rule his brother had told him.Ⓕ

Is box A striped?Ⓖ

So is the frog inside box A?Ⓗ

Tom looked at box B.

Is box B striped?Ⓘ

So is the frog inside box B?Ⓙ

Tom looked at box C.Ⓚ After looking at all the boxes, Tom opened box B.Ⓛ

Did a frog hop out of box B?Ⓜ

Turn to the next page and you will see what happened.Ⓝ 🌸 4 ERRORS 🌸

LESSON 2

A

1	2	3	4	5
field	listen	football	full	gray
straight	listened	here's	grow	water
point	lesson	pull	fact	cover
whole	wear	grew	facts	covered
wash	ice cream	forest		
together				

6
Vocabulary words
1. strange
2. wise

B

Things People Eat

The story that you'll read today tells about things that people eat. Some things are good for you and some things are not good for you. Here's the rule: **Sweet things like apples and grapes are good for you.** Ⓐ

Sweet things like cake and candy are not very good for you. Ⓑ

C

Tom Gets Fat Ⓐ

Tom was a little boy. He was smaller than the other boys. He wanted to be big so that he could play football. Ⓑ But he was too small. Ⓒ One day his brother said, "If you want to get big, you have to eat more. Here's the rule: **The more you eat, the bigger you will get.**" Ⓓ

Tom wanted to get big. So he started to eat. Ⓔ He ate cake. He ate ice cream. He ate hot dogs. He ate and ate and ate and ate. Ⓕ

The more Tom ate, the bigger he got. He did not get taller. He got fatter. Ⓖ ✻ 2 ERRORS ✻

Soon Tom was so fat that he could not wear his shirts or his pants. He had to get new shirts and pants. Soon Tom was so fat that he could not run. Ⓗ He could not run, so he could not play football. Tom was not very happy. ✻ 4 ERRORS ✻

LESSON 3

1	2	3	4	5
together	point	forest	grew	**Vocabulary**
wash	pointed	grow	moop	**words**
washed	straight	listened	gray	**1.** path
whole	field	full	water	**2.** pet
	fields	here's	facts	**3.** wise
				4. strange

B

Make-Believe Animals

The story you'll read today tells about animals called moops. Moops are make-believe animals. That means there really are not any moops. Ⓐ

Here's another make-believe animal.

What parts of the animal are make-believe? Ⓑ
Here's a real animal. Ⓒ

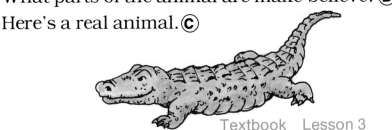

Bob and Don Find Moops Ⓐ

Don and Bob lived near a strange forest. Ⓑ There were many strange animals in the forest. One strange animal was a moop. Ⓒ Moops were little animals with long hair. They made very good pets. Ⓓ

One day Don and Bob went out to get pet moops. Ⓔ On the path they met a wise old man. The wise old man said, "A moop makes a good pet. But do not cut a moop's hair. Here's the rule about a moop: **The more you cut its hair, the faster its hair grows.**" Ⓕ

Don listened to the old man. But Bob did not listen. Ⓖ 🔷 c cппопо 🔷

Don found a pet moop and Bob found a pet moop. Don took his pet moop home and put it in a box. Ⓗ Bob took his pet moop home and looked at it. Bob said, "The hair on this moop is too long. So I will cut it." ❶ Bob started to cut the moop's hair, but the hair started to grow back. So Bob cut more hair. But the more he cut the hair, the faster the hair grew.

Soon the moop's hair was so long that it filled the room. Soon the hair was so long that Bob could not find his moop. Ⓙ

Don kept his moop for years. Don had a lot of fun with his moop. But Bob did not have fun with his moop. Ⓚ He never found his moop. All he could see was a room full of hair. ❋ 5 ERRORS ❋

LESSON 4

A

1	2	3	4	5
canoe	away	fields	pointed	figure
forward	apart	covered	gray	paddle
move	across	water	together	paddling
arrow	around	facts	straight	boat
Indian	another	washed	whole	
large				

B

Forests

In the story you will read today, Don walks through a forest. Here are facts about forests:

- A forest is a place where many tall trees grow close together. Ⓐ
- Forest trees block the light from the sun. So the inside of the forest is very dark. Ⓑ
- You can tell a forest tree by looking at it. **Forest trees are very tall and straight.** Ⓒ

- **Trees that grow in fields are not tall and straight.** Ⓓ

C   Don Washes the White Spot Ⓐ

Don had a pretty white coat. But he didn't like white coats. He wanted a gray coat.Ⓑ Don said, "I'll buy a gray coat." So he started to walk to town.Ⓒ He had to walk through the strange forest to get to town.Ⓓ Don met the wise old man on the path through the forest. Don told the wise old man, "I'm on my way to get a gray coat."

The wise old man said, "I will give you a gray coat." The wise old man held up a pretty gray coat.   2 ERRORS

The coat had one little white spot on it. The old man pointed to the spot and said, "Do not try to wash this spot away. Here's the rule: **The more you wash this spot, the bigger it will get.**" Ⓔ

*Don did not listen to the old man. **F** Don took the pretty gray coat home. Then he said to himself, "I don't like that little spot on the coat. I will wash it away." **G**

So Don got some soap and water. Then he started to wash the spot. He washed a little bit and the spot got a little bigger. Don washed some more. And the white spot got bigger. Don washed and washed and washed. And the spot got bigger and bigger and bigger. The more Don washed, the* bigger the spot got.

Soon the white spot was so big that it covered the whole coat. The whole coat was white. Now Don did not have a white coat and a gray coat. He had two white coats. Don said, "I hate white coats." ❇ 6 ERRORS ❇

LESSON 5

A

1	2	3	4	5
grow	figure	Indian	boat	come
flow	canoe	Indians	paddle	coming
show	arrow	large	wave	out
arrow	move	paddling	waves	dugout
	moving	middle		

6	7
burn	**Vocabulary words**
burned	**1.** forward
birch	**2.** pull
frame	

B

Don Cuts Trees Ⓐ

The old man told Don, "Cut down some trees. And cut them into big logs. Ⓑ But here's the rule: **Do not cut down any trees from the fields. Cut trees from the forest.**" Ⓒ

Don did not know what a forest is. He did not know what a field is. Ⓓ Don went out and cut down trees. He took the logs back to the old man.

When the old man looked at the logs, he was very mad. He pointed to some of the logs and said, "These logs are not from the forest. These logs are from the field." Ⓔ ✸ 2 ERRORS ✸

If you are very smart, you can figure out which logs are from the field and which logs are from the forest. Ⓕ ✸ 4 ERRORS ✸

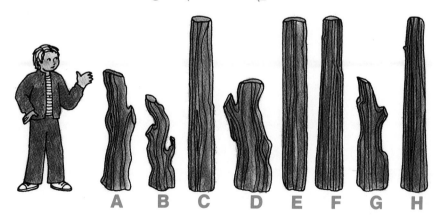

A   B   C   D   E   F   G   H

LESSON 6

1	2	3	4	5
lily	moving	flow	boat	part
hurry	arrow	flows	paddling	parts
pretty	canoe	coming	birch	sheet
hungry	show	paddle	dugout	sheets
	large	middle	burned	frame

6
Vocabulary words

1. waves
2. bark
3. pull
4. forward

B

HOW TO PADDLE A CANOE Ⓐ

*A canoe is a small boat. Ⓑ You use a paddle to make a canoe move. In the picture, a man is standing next to a paddle. Ⓒ

Here are the rules about paddling a canoe.
You grab the paddle with your hands. One
hand is on the top of the paddle. The other hand
is in the middle of the paddle.Ⓓ

You hold the paddle in front of you. You
reach out and put the paddle in the water. Then
you pull back on the paddle. You pull hard.Ⓔ

When you* pull the paddle back, the canoe
moves forward.Ⓕ ❋ 2 ERRORS ❋

These pictures show how to paddle.

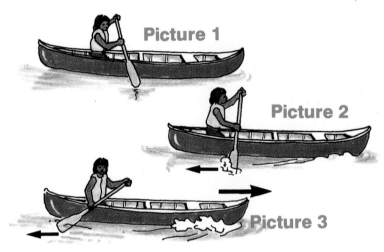

Picture 1

Picture 2

Picture 3

Touch picture 1.Ⓖ The girl is holding the paddle in front of her. She is holding the paddle with two hands. One hand is on top of the paddle. Her other hand is in the middle of the paddle.Ⓗ

Picture 2 shows the paddle in the water. The girl is starting to pull the paddle back. The arrow below the paddle shows which way the paddle is moving in the water.Ⓘ

Picture 3 shows the girl pulling the paddle back very hard. The arrow below the paddle shows which way her paddle is moving. The big arrow over the canoe shows which way the canoe is moving.

The paddle is moving this way: ⟵

The canoe is moving this way: ⟶ Ⓙ

Look at the waves coming off the front of the canoe. Ⓚ The front of the canoe is making waves because the canoe is moving through the water. Ⓛ **The faster the canoe moves, the bigger the waves get.** Ⓜ

Look at the picture below. One of the canoes is going very fast. Figure out which canoe that is. Ⓝ

One canoe is not moving at all. Which canoe is that? Ⓞ ❋ 6 ERRORS ❋

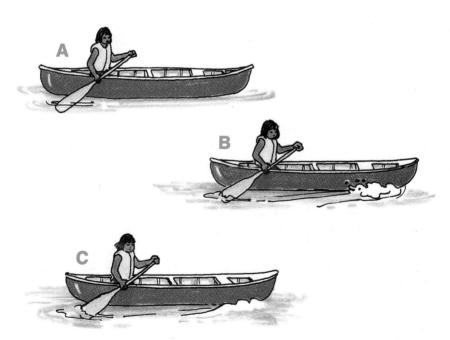

LESSON 7

A

1	2	3	4	5
forest	Indians	dugout	sheets	paddle
shore	lily	parts	parts	paddled
short	lilies	hungry	frame	rang
forward	hurry	hungrier	birch	color
	Indian	burned	count	colors

6

pull
pulled
remember
remembered

7

Vocabulary words

bark

B

Indian Canoes Ⓐ

People have had canoes for a long, long time. Indians who lived near water made canoes. Ⓑ Some Indians made dugout canoes and some made canoes from bark. Ⓒ

Here's how Indians made dugout canoes. Ⓓ Dugout canoes are made from logs. Ⓔ So the Indians cut down a tree that was tall and straight.(F) They cut a long log from the forest tree.

They made a fire on the top of the log. As the fire burned, they cut away the parts that had burned.(G)

The Indians cut away the parts that had burned until the inside of the log looked like this:(H)   ❄ 2 ERRORS ❄

Indians made bark canoes from the bark of birch trees.(I) That bark comes off birch trees in sheets.(J)

First the Indians made a frame that looked like this:**Ⓚ**

After they made the frame, they covered the frame with birch bark.**Ⓛ**

When the canoe was done, it was very fast and it was very easy to lift.**Ⓜ** The picture below shows a canoe made from birch bark.**Ⓝ**

❀ 4 ERRORS ❀

LESSON 8

A

1	2	3	4
hungrier	rang	pulled	**Vocabulary**
count	Jane	sink	**words**
dong	drink	remembered	shore
short	colors	shaft	
paddled	drank		

B

Don Makes the Fish Too Hungry Ⓐ

Don said, "I think I will go fishing." Ⓑ So
Don took his fishing pole and went to the big

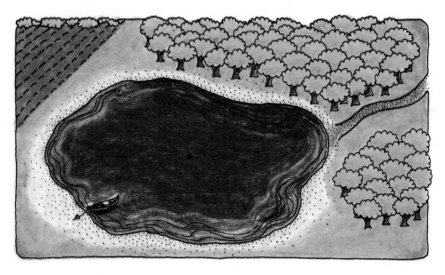

lake that was next to the strange forest.Ⓒ The wise old man let him use a canoe. Don got in the canoe and went out to the middle of the lake.Ⓓ Don fished and fished and fished, but he did not get any fish.

He paddled the canoe back to the shore. He was mad.Ⓔ He didn't get one fish.Ⓕ The wise old man was standing on the shore. The wise old man held up a bell. ❋ 2 ERRORS ❋

The old man said, "When you ring this bell, the fish get hungry. Here's the rule: **The more you ring this bell, the hungrier the fish get.**Ⓖ But remember, if you ring this bell too much, the fish will get very, very hungry."Ⓗ

Don took the bell and paddled back out to the middle of the lake.ⒾHe rang the bell: "Dong, dong."Ⓙ Then Don put his fishing line into the water. Before you could count to ten, a fish was on his line.Ⓚ Don pulled the fish into the canoe. Then he took the bell and rang it again and again: "Dong, dong, dong, dong, dong."Ⓛ Don put his fishing line back into the water. Before you could count to five, he had another fish.Ⓜ

Don picked up the bell and rang it fifty times. Ⓝ The fish got so hungry that they jumped out of the water. They swam this way and that way. Then they started to eat everything they could find. Ⓞ They found the canoe. And they started to eat it. The canoe went down and Don was in the water. Ⓟ Then the fish ate Don's fishing pole. Then they ate his fishing line. Then they ate the bell. At last, they ate Don's shirt and pants.

When Don swam to the shore, the wise old man said to him, "Don, you must listen when I tell you a rule. I told you not to ring the bell too much." ❋ 7 ERRORS ❋

LESSON 9

1
cloth
write
erase
construction

2
ink
sink
sank
drank
drink

3
large
short
apart
apartment
lilies

4
creep
sheet
Jane
colors

5
pulled
remembered
write
writing
shaft

6
Vocabulary words
1. hurry
2. cloth

B

Water Lilies

Today's story tells about water lilies. Water lilies are very pretty plants that grow in the water. Ⓐ

Here are facts about water lilies:

- Water lilies have large flat leaves that float on the water. Ⓑ
- Water lilies have flowers that are as big around as a dish. Ⓒ
- Some water lilies are yellow. Some are pink, and some are white. Ⓓ

Here is a picture of some water lilies. Ⓔ

C   Jane Takes a Short Cut Ⓐ

Jane was in a hurry to get to the town of Creep. This town was on the other side of the lake. The road to Creep went around the lake. First the road went through the strange forest. Then it went past a farm. Then it went through a little forest. At last it came to the town of Creep. Ⓡ

Jane ran from her house to the strange forest. Then she stopped to rest. Ⓒ The wise old man came up to her and asked, "Where are you going?"

She told him. Ⓓ ✳ 2 ERRORS ✳

The old man said, "A much faster way to get to the town of Creep is to go across the lake." Ⓔ

"But I don't have a boat," Jane said.

*Then the old man said, "I don't have my good canoe anymore. Ⓕ But I have another canoe that you may use. That canoe has a hole in the front. Here's the rule about that canoe: **If you sit near the back, the canoe won't sink.**" Ⓖ

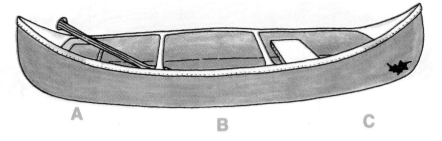

"I will remember that rule," Jane said. Ⓗ Jane got in the canoe and began to paddle. As she paddled through the water lilies, a very pretty water lily got stuck to the front of the canoe, Jane saw the water lily and said to* herself, "I would love to have that flower." Ⓘ

But did Jane go to the front of the canoe? No, she remembered what the wise old man had told her. Ⓙ

She paddled faster and faster. When she was in the middle of the lake, she wanted something to drink. She did not want to drink the water from the lake because it was not clean. But she saw a bottle of water in the front of the canoe. The bottle was full. **K** But did Jane go to the front of the canoe? No, she remembered what the wise old man had said.

She paddled all the way to the other side of the lake. She pulled the canoe as far onto the shore as she could. **L** Then she grabbed the bottle of water from the front of the canoe. She opened the bottle and drank.

Then she ran to the town of Creep. She was not late. **M** ❀ 8 ERRORS ❀

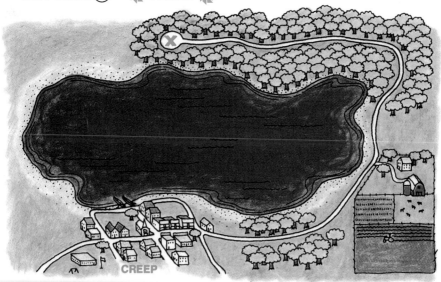

CREEP

LESSON 10

1
Joe Williams
Mary Williams
centimeter
thought

2
dance
prance
pencil
fence

3
construction
erase
eraser
writing

4
apartment
ink
shaft
flows

5
tip
tipped
brush
brushes
shape

6
Vocabulary words
cloth

B

Felt-Tipped Pens (A)

The story you'll read in the next lesson is about a felt-tipped pen. (B) Here are facts about felt-tipped pens:

- Felt-tipped pens have tips that are made of felt. (C) Felt is a kind of cloth. (D)
- The shaft of the pen is filled with ink. (E) A shaft is the long part of the pen that you hold when you write. (F)
- The ink flows down to the tip. (G) Ink is wet. The tip is made of cloth. So when ink gets on the tip, the tip gets wet. (H)   ❋ 2 ERRORS ❋
- Most felt-tipped pens do not have an eraser. (I) Ink is not easy to erase. (J) What kind of writing tool does have an eraser? (K)

❋ 4 ERRORS ❋

LESSON 11

1	2	3	4
waddle	Joe Williams	apartment	dance
beautiful	Mary Williams	pencil	dancing
fault	rule	shaft	around
diet	ruler	ink	fence
lose	eraser	centimeter	prance
heavy			

5

Vocabulary words

1. construction

2. thoughts

3. hard hat

B

Joe Williams Wants a New Job Ⓐ

Joe Williams was a felt-tipped pen. He had a wide tip and his color was bright red. Ⓑ Joe's job was construction. He worked with other members of the construction team—pencils,

paints, other pens, brushes, and erasers.Ⓒ
Their construction job was to make pictures.Ⓓ

All day long, Joe worked with the others.
They worked very fast. First, Joe would be
sitting next to the other pens. Then somebody
would pick him up, make a few marks with
him, and toss him back with the other pens.

✳ 2 ERRORS ✳

The work was hard, and everybody on the
construction team was glad when it was time
for lunch.Ⓔ The members of the team would sit
and talk about the picture they were making.
Then, at one o'clock, work would start again,
and it would keep going until the end of the day.

After the work was done, Joe would take off the hard hat he wore for the construction jobs. Ⓕ Joe would go to his apartment. He lived in the desk with his wife, Mary, who worked as a number one pencil. Ⓖ

Every day, the same thing happened. Joe worked on construction, laying down red lines and red marks. Then he went home. One day, Joe said to himself, "I'm tired of being a felt-tipped pen. I'm tired of laying down red lines. I want a new job." Ⓗ

When Joe told his wife that he was thinking of taking up a new job, she said, "Don't be silly, Joe. What else can you do?" Ⓘ Joe looked at himself. He couldn't work as an eraser because he didn't have an eraser. Ⓙ He couldn't work as a pencil holder, because he didn't have the right shape. Ⓚ He couldn't work as a sheet of paper. Ⓛ

He said to himself, "Let's face it, Joe. You're just made to be a red felt-tipped pen." Ⓜ Then he said, "But I must be able to do something else."

Joe felt sad, but he didn't stop thinking about a new job. Ⓝ ✳ 7 ERRORS ✳

LESSON 12

A

1
exercise
supermarket
healthy
standard
spa

2
Jokey
heavy
hardly
ugly
curly

3
fence
shouldn't
lose
diet

4
ugly
ugliest
fault
beautiful

5
waddle
waddled
prance
dancing

6
round
centimeter
around
ruler

7

Vocabulary words

1. waddle

2. thoughts

B

CENTIMETERS

The story you'll read today talks about centimeters. Here is a rule about centimeters: **All centimeters are the same size.** (A)

Every line in this row is one centimeter long: (B)

Every line in this row is two centimeters long:

Every line in this row is three centimeters long:

C

Joe Williams Gets a New Job (A)

Every night, Joe went home and thought about jobs that he might do, but he didn't come up with any good thoughts. Then one night, Joe had a good thought. He was watching his wife, Mary. She was singing to herself, and she was dancing. When a number one pencil dances, she makes a little line on the floor. Then she jumps and makes another little line right next to the first line. As Joe watched her make these lines, he jumped up from the chair and jumped across the floor. "I've got it," he yelled. "I've got it!" Ⓑ

✿ 2 ERRORS ✿

Mary stopped dancing and looked at Joe. "What are you thinking?"

Joe said, "I want you to make marks on me. Make marks that are one centimeter apart. Make marks all down the side of my shaft. If I have those marks on my shaft, I can work as a ruler." Ⓒ

Mary laughed. **D** Then she stopped laughing and said, "Say, maybe it will work. Let's see." **E**

She made the marks on Joe's side. When she was done, Joe jumped up and looked at himself. "Wow, that's nice," he said. He kept turning around and looking at himself. "I'll be the only round ruler on the construction team."

The next day, Joe didn't line up with the other pens. He went over with the rulers. **F**

One ruler said, "What do you think you're doing here, pen?"

"I'm now a ruler," Joe said.

Another ruler said, "We'll soon find out if you're really a ruler. It's just about time to work."

Pretty soon, somebody picked up Joe and said, "Let's see how this round ruler works." The person used Joe as a ruler. "This round ruler works very well," the person said. And from that day on, Joe had a new job. He was a round ruler. **G** 🌸 6 ERRORS 🌸

LESSON 13

A

1	2	3	4
supermarket	roll	heavy	fence
hallway	rolling	waddled	ugly
cardboard	Jokey	beautiful	ugliest
sidewalk	shouldn't	hardly	healthy
baseball	lose	diet	spa
tiptoes			

5	6	7
stretch	prance	**Vocabulary words**
stretched	pranced	1. table scraps
standard	prancer	2. exercise
poodle	curly	3. fault
poodles		4. health spa
		5. waddle

B

Facts about Beagles

The story you're going to read today is about a beagle. Here are facts about beagles:Ⓐ
- Beagles are dogs.Ⓑ
- Beagles are very short.Ⓒ
- Beagles have short hair and short legs. Ⓓ
- Beagles have long ears and long tails.Ⓔ
- Beagles have coats that are three colors: black, white, and brown.Ⓕ

C

Jokey, the Fat Beagle Ⓐ

There was a beagle named Jokey who was very fat. He was fat because he ate everything. He ate the kinds of things that other beagles eat—things like dog food and bones and table scraps. But Jokey ate things that other dogs don't eat—things like bottle caps, mops, and pencils.Ⓑ

The people who owned Jokey got madder and madder as the dog got fatter and fatter.Ⓒ The dog was getting fatter because the dog was eating things that he shouldn't eat.

"You are a fat dog," they would say.

❋ 2 ERRORS ❋

One day, Jokey waddled out into his yard.Ⓓ He was very, very fat because he had just eaten a broom. His belly was touching the

ground. He was so heavy that he could hardly move.

A black cat jumped onto the fence of the yard. The cat told Jokey, "You're about the fattest thing I've ever seen. If I looked like you, I'd never eat again."Ⓔ

There was a rat peeking through the fence on the other side of the yard. "That's right," the rat yelled. "Everybody thinks I look bad, but I look good next to you."Ⓕ

Jokey tried to pull in his big belly so he wouldn't look so fat. It didn't work. His belly was still touching the ground. "I can't help it if I'm fat," Jokey said. "It's not my fault."Ⓖ

"Wrong," the cat said. "It is your fault. Don't you know the rule: **The more you eat, the fatter you get.**Ⓗ If you don't eat as much, you won't be so fat."Ⓘ

The rat yelled out, "Everybody knows that. If you want to lose that fat, stop eating so much. Go on a diet."Ⓙ

"A diet?" Jokey asked. "What's a diet?"Ⓚ

"I just told you," the rat said. "When you cut down on your eating, you go on a diet."Ⓛ

✿ 6 ERRORS ✿

LESSON 14

A

1	2	3	4
weight	baseball	exercise	supermarket
sugar	rolling	exercises	hallway
toward	tiptoes	poodles	standard
	healthy	prancer	curly
	stretched	pranced	

5	6	7
centimeter	catch	cardboard
hour	hungry	quit
meter	high	quitting
slob	lost	sidewalk
slobber	careful	

8
Vocabulary words

1. trash
2. prance
3. exercise
4. health spa

B

Facts about Poodles

In today's story you're going to read about poodles. Poodles are dogs that come in all sizes. The ones in the story are standard poodles, which are the biggest poodles. Ⓐ Standard poodles are much bigger than beagles. Ⓑ Here are facts about standard poodles:

- Standard poodles are the same color all over. Ⓒ
- Standard poodles have very curly hair. Ⓓ
- Standard poodles have ears that hang down and they have a cut-off tail. Ⓔ

C

Jokey Goes to a Health Spa Ⓐ

A rat and a cat were telling Jokey that he should go on a diet. Ⓑ The cat was making fun of dogs. Ⓒ

"Don't say bad things about dogs," Jokey said. "Or I'll jump up on that fence and take a bite out of your tail."

The cat stretched out on the fence and let

her black tail hang down. She laughed and then said, "Come on, let's see you leap up and grab this tail." Ⓓ

Here's what Jokey planned to do: Show his teeth, run to the fence, leap up in the air, and take a big bite out of the cat's tail. Ⓔ ✳ 2 ERRORS ✳

But here's what Jokey did: He showed his teeth. He waddled to the fence. He looked up at the tail. He bent his legs. Then he showed his teeth some more. Ⓕ

*The rat was laughing and rolling around. "That beagle is so fat," the rat said, "he can't jump one centimeter off the ground." Ⓖ

The next day Jokey went to a health spa. Ⓗ This spa was near a supermarket, but Jokey didn't stop in the back of the supermarket to go through the trash cans. He went straight to the spa. The dogs who ran the spa were poodles, who pranced around with their heads up in the air. They seemed to be walking on their tiptoes. One of them pranced* up to Jokey, looked at him, and said, "Well, I'm not sure we can help any dog as fat and ugly as you, but we'll try." The poodle said, "Follow me," and pranced down the hallway.

Jokey tried to prance after the poodle. ❶
He put his tail straight up in the air to make
himself look more like a prancer. But his belly
still dragged on the floor.

The poodle led Jokey into an exercise room.
Another poodle with white curly hair pranced
up to them. The room was filled with other fat
dogs doing exercises. Jokey, of course, was the
fattest dog in the exercise room. Ⓙ ✳ 7 ERRORS ✳

LESSON 15

1	2	3	4	5
zero	quitting	catch	high	weight
month	hour	cardboard	lost	hadn't
different	meters	evening	careful	nearly
reward	slobber	hungry	toward	tease
	slobbering	hungrier	sugar	teasing

6
Vocabulary words
slim and trim

METERS

The story you're going to read today tells about meters. Ⓐ We use meters to measure how long things are.

Here are facts about meters:

- A standard poodle is about one meter long. Ⓑ

- A meter is 1 hundred centimeters long. Ⓒ

The picture shows a person holding a stick that is one meter long.

Jokey Starts His Diet Ⓐ

The white poodle in the exercise room gave Jokey some good news and some bad news. Here was the good news: "You can be slim and trim in no time at all." Ⓑ

Here was the bad news: "You'll have to run for one hour each day. You'll have to do exercises for another hour, and you'll have to stop eating." Ⓒ

Jokey tried. At first, Jokey couldn't run for an hour. He couldn't even run five meters. So he walked for about three blocks. Then he fell over, panting and slobbering. (D) �֎ 2 ERRORS ✷

Next, Jokey tried to do exercises for an hour. His problem was that he couldn't do any of the exercises. He couldn't catch a ball. He couldn't do push-ups. He couldn't play catch-your-tail. He couldn't even see his tail. (E)

Then came the hardest part—not eating. (F) Picture that fat beagle when he left the spa. He had to walk next to the supermarket. There were the smells of bread and meat and fish and candy and milk and cheese. And there were the smells of other things that were great to eat— trash, paper, tin cans, and cardboard boxes. (G)

But Jokey walked past the supermarket without stopping. And that evening he didn't eat any socks or rugs or trash. He just sat around, trying not to feel hungry. (H)

The next day, he was so hungry that he was ready to say, "I quit this diet." But there was one thing that kept him from quitting. His belly was no longer dragging on the ground. When he walked into the spa that day, his belly was one centimeter off the floor. The diet was working. (I)

✷ 6 ERRORS ✷

LESSON 16

A

1	2	3	4
Santa	within	farther	careful
push	fireplace	while	carefully
reindeer	gentlemen	drank	high
shoulder	without	sidewalk	lost
		baseball	trash

5	6	7	8
exercised	pointer	chimney	**Vocabulary**
sugar	different	month	**words**
toward	nearly	pull	1. proud
zero	ant	pulled	2. flick
hadn't	antler	morning	3. weight
			4. reward
			5. tease
			6. dash

B
Diets

You've been reading about diets.

The rule that the rat gave for a diet is: **When you cut down on your eating, you go on a diet.** Ⓐ

The rat told one way to go on a diet. Here's the big rule about diets: **When you follow a new way of eating, you go on a diet.** Ⓑ

Some people follow a new way of eating by eating more. They go on a diet to put on weight. Ⓒ

Some people must stop eating some things, like sugar. They follow a new way of eating by going on a sugar-free diet.

Some people are like Jokey. They follow a new way of eating to lose weight. They must cut down on their eating. Ⓓ

Some people follow a new way of eating to stay healthy. They are in good shape, and they eat carefully to stay in good shape. Their diet makes sure they eat foods that are good for them. Ⓔ

C

JOKEY GOES OFF HIS DIET ⒶⒶ

Jokey's diet worked the first day. Ⓑ The next day, Jokey said to himself, "I really want to be slim, so I will stay on my diet for a while." And he did. That day, he walked and he exercised. He walked farther than he had walked the day before, and he was able to do more exercises. Jokey went straight home without stopping at the supermarket. When he got home, he drank water and drank water until he couldn't drink any more. Ⓒ

You know how far Jokey's belly was from the floor at the end of the first day. Ⓓ ❈ 2 ERRORS ❈

At the end of the next day, his belly was one centimeter farther from the floor. Ⓔ

But on the fifth day of his diet, Jokey went off his diet. Ⓕ He left the spa and kept his head high as he walked past the supermarket. When he was almost home, he saw a baseball on the sidewalk. It looked very good. He couldn't stand it and—chomp, chomp. Ⓖ Jokey ate the baseball. Then he went sort of crazy. He went down the alley and ate trash—lots of it. He ate

bags and cardboard boxes and everything he could find. He ate until his belly was one centimeter from the ground.Ⓗ Then he couldn't hold any more, and he waddled toward his home. On the way, he saw the black cat.

"Here comes that fat dog," she said. "I hear that they keep you at the spa so that the other dogs will feel skinny. I hear that one dog lost four pounds just from laughing at you."

"Stop teasing me," Jokey said, "or I'll take a bite out of your tail."❶

"Here it is," the cat said, and she held her tail high in the air. "Just run right over here and take a big bite."

Jokey didn't even try. He knew that the cat would be gone before he could move five steps. So he tried to pull in his belly and not listen to the cat. As Jokey walked home, he said to himself, "I'll never go off my diet again."Ⓙ

✿ 7 ERRORS ✿

LESSON 17

A

1	2	3	4
aunt	teased	pointer	reward
circus	gentlemen	nearly	within
famous	hadn't	zero	weight
expensive	Santa	month	high
restaurant	reindeer	different	chimney
human			

5	6	7	8
pushed	antler	without	bread
shoulder	antlers	waxed	insect
pulled	fireplace	praise	male
morning	world	during	female
flicked	worm	match	eight

9
Vocabulary words

1. elf
2. push
3. pull
4. compared
5. proud
6. flick

B

Facts about Pointers

The story you'll read today tells about another kind of dog. These dogs are pointers. Here are facts about pointers:

- Pointers are about the same size as standard poodles.(A)
- Pointers have short hair, long ears that hang down, and long tails.(B)
- Pointers are used as hunting dogs.(C)
  When pointers are very close to birds that are hiding in the grass, they point.
  Here's how a pointer points:
- The pointer holds one of its front paws off the ground.
- The pointer stands very still.
- The pointer looks at the spot where the bird is.(D)

C

Jokey, the Proud Beagle Ⓐ

When Jokey went off his diet, he filled his belly and gained weight. He lost that weight the next day. After he stayed on his diet three more days, he was starting to look slim. Ⓑ

Beagles have short hair, and when a beagle is very skinny, you can see its rib bones very clearly. Ⓒ Jokey was still so fat that you couldn't see all his ribs, but when he pulled in his belly, his ribs made little tiny marks in his fur. Ⓓ And Jokey pulled in his belly all the time. He was proud of himself. Ⓔ ❋ 2 ERRORS ❋

He could do things he hadn't been able to do for years. He could chase his tail. He could catch a ball. He could do twenty push-ups. He could jump ten centimeters off the ground. Ⓕ That wasn't very high compared to what some of the other dogs could do. One pointer could jump one meter off the ground, and the white poodle who ran the exercise room could jump nearly two meters. But ten centimeters off the ground is a lot better than zero centimeters off the ground. Ⓖ

So Jokey stayed with his diet—for two weeks, for three weeks, for one month, for two months. And at the end of two months, you should have seen him. You would never know it was the same dog.Ⓗ He walked on his tiptoes. His belly was very, very small, and his chest stuck out with a row of ribs showing on each side. His legs had big muscles and so did his arms.Ⓘ

When he walked into the spa, everybody smiled and said, "Hi, Jokey."Ⓙ On the wall were pictures of Jokey. One showed him before his diet and the other showed him now. Jokey looked very different.Ⓚ Jokey could now jump nearly two meters off the ground. He could run for an hour without stopping. And he was nearly as fast as the white poodle. Jokey felt so good that he didn't ever want to go back to eating like a slob.Ⓛ

Jokey's biggest reward came one day when he was in his yard, doing exercises. The black cat was on the fence. The cat was saying, "For a dog, you don't look bad. But all dogs are ugly."

"Watch out," Jokey said, "or I'll jump up on that fence and take a bite out of your tail." Ⓜ

The cat flicked her tail. "Here it is, beagle,
Come and . . ."

Before the cat could say another word,
Jokey dashed across the yard and jumped onto
the fence. He showed his teeth. Then he smiled
and said, "This time I'll let you go, but if you
ever tease me again, I'm going to take a bite out
of your tail."

That cat never teased Jokey again.

🌸 9 ERRORS 🌸

LESSON 18

A

1	2	3	4
Russia	chimney	reindeer	world
taught	shoulder	morning	worms
instead	pushed	Santa	restaurant
directions	pulled	fireplace	expensive
instructions	eight	antlers	waxed

5	6	7	8
praise	agreed	human	**Vocabulary words**
during	insect	aunt	1. males
match	circus	famous	2. females
bread	circuses	elves	3. elf
			4. pull
			5. push

B   Facts about Reindeer

The make-believe story you'll read today tells about Santa and his reindeer.Ⓐ Santa's reindeer fly, but real reindeer cannot fly.Ⓑ Here are some facts about real reindeer:

- A male reindeer is about two meters long and one meter tall at the shoulder.Ⓒ
- Reindeer live in places that are very cold.Ⓓ
- Both male reindeer and female reindeer have antlers.Ⓔ Antlers are horns that grow from the top of the reindeer's head.
- Reindeer are used to pull sleds.
- Reindeer are also used to give milk.Ⓕ

C   Santa Gets StuckⒶ

One year Santa was very fat. He was with eight elves on top of a roof. He took his sack of gifts and started down a chimney very fast.Ⓑ But suddenly, he stopped. He was stuck.Ⓒ He pushed with his hands and pulled with his feet, but it was no use. Ⓓ He called to Max, the elf who made the big toys. Max told him, "Pull with your hands and push with your feet." Ⓔ That didn't work. Santa called to Bix, the elf who made the little toys. Bix told him, "Push with your hands and pull with your feet." Ⓕ But Santa tried that again, and it still didn't work.

❀ 2 ERRORS ❀

Max and Bix went inside the house. They talked to each other and then told Santa about their plan. They put three elves inside the chimney, pushing up on Santa. Three more elves were on top of the roof, pulling up on a rope that Santa was holding. The rope went to the sled, where eight reindeer were ready to pull also. Ⓖ

Max said, "Everybody go when I count to three. One . . . two . . . three."

The elves under Santa pushed up on his bottom. The elves on top of the chimney pulled up as hard as they could on the rope. Eight reindeer took off into the night sky. And it worked. Santa popped out of the chimney like a cork. Ⓗ

The next morning, the people who lived in
the house came down to the fireplace to find out
what Santa had left for them. There was a big
bag of gifts. But there was something else. The
little girl who lived in the house said, "I wonder
why Santa left this pair of big red pants. Who
are they for?" ① ❋ 6 ERRORS ❋

LESSON 19

A

1
tomorrow
surprise
great
introduced

2
Martha Jumpjump
Henry Ouch
Carl Goodscratch
directions
restaurant

3
instructions
world
spider
aunt

4
during
famous
bread
insects
change

5
Russia
lady
ladies
welcome
circuses

6
twist
twisted
taught
juggle

7
instead
without
human
row
expensive

8
Vocabulary words
line-up

B

Facts about Fleas

You'll read about fleas in today's story. Here are some facts about fleas:

- Fleas are insects.
  All insects have six legs.
  So fleas have six legs. Ⓐ
- Fleas bite and suck blood. Ⓑ
- A row of about five big fleas is one centimeter long. Ⓒ
- Different kinds of fleas live on different kinds of animals.

Cat fleas like to live on cats. Cat fleas are different from dog fleas. Dog fleas are different from human fleas. Human fleas are different from rat fleas. Ⓓ

The picture below shows a dog flea. Ⓔ

real size

Aunt Fanny's Flea Circus Ⓐ

Aunt Fanny's Flea Circus was formed in 1963. The circus had a great line-up of acts.Ⓑ Aunt Fanny had the most famous fleas in the world. One act was Carl Goodscratch, who dove 48 centimeters into two drops of water.Ⓒ When Carl did his dive, the people watching the show would sit without making a sound. Then they would cheer and stamp their feet.Ⓓ Another act that crowds loved was Martha Jumpjump, who skipped rope while walking with one leg on a high wire.Ⓔ (The high wire was really a spider web that had been waxed so that Martha wouldn't stick to it.)Ⓕ   ✸ 2 ERRORS ✸

*Then there was the French flea, Henry Ouch, the flea who trained rats. He would get into a cage with four or five rats and have them do all kinds of tricks. If they did not do what he told them to do, he would jump on their backs and bite them.Ⓖ

Aunt Fanny's Flea Circus went around the world, bringing in big crowds and making lots of money. But in 1971, Aunt Fanny and the

fleas started to fight a lot. The fleas said that
Aunt Fanny was hogging* all the fame.(H) Aunt
Fanny said that she could do what she wanted
because she owned the circus. You can see why
the fleas would get mad at Fanny. After each
show, people would come up and praise Fanny.
"Great show, Fanny," they would say. The only
thing Fanny did during the show was wave a
stick at the fleas. The fleas did the real work.(I)

Also, Aunt Fanny hogged all the money.(J)
She kept the poor fleas locked in a little
cardboard matchbox while she lived in
expensive apartments.(K) She fed them dry
bread while she ate at the best restaurants.(L)
She put thousands of dollars into the bank, but
she didn't give the fleas a dime.(M)

One night the fleas made up their minds that things had to change.

"She's treating us like worms," Carl said.  "Are we going to take that?"

"No," all the other fleas agreed. "Things must change." 7 ERRORS

LESSON 20

A

1	2	3	4	5
pillow	o<u>a</u>	great	ladies	taught
rough	r<u>oa</u>d	greatest	welcome	twisted
wart	s<u>oa</u>k	tomorrow	circuses	gentlemen
suit	t<u>oa</u>d	change	surprise	juggle
	b<u>oa</u>t	Russia	introduced	
	t<u>oa</u>st			

6

crowd
instead
directions
sometimes
instructions

7

goldfish
family
large
tadpole

8

Vocabulary words

introduce

B

Directions on a Map

You are going to read about 4 directions: north, south, east, and west.Ⓐ Maps always show: north on the top.

south on the bottom.

east on this side: ⟶

west on this side: ⟵   Ⓑ

If something on a map goes north, it goes this way: ↑   Ⓒ

If something on a map goes south, it goes this way: ↓   Ⓓ

C

Facts about Flea Circuses⒜

When we left Aunt Fanny in the last story, the fleas were mad at her. Name three things they were mad about.⒝

The fleas in the story talk, so we know they are make-believe fleas.⒞ But there are such things as flea circuses. And these flea circuses do have fleas that put on acts.⒟ Here are some facts about flea circuses:

- Most fleas that are used in flea circuses come from Russia.⒠
- Fleas have been taught to juggle things.⒡
- Fleas have been taught to jump through hoops.⒢
- Some fleas have been taught to pull things that weigh a hundred times as much as a flea.⒣ ❉ 2 ERRORS ❉
- The first trick a flea must be taught is to walk instead of hop.⒤ Fleas like to take a great hop to go from place to place. But they can walk.

After they have been taught to walk, they can be taught to walk on a high wire or to pull a cart.⒥ ❉ 6 ERRORS ❉

LESSON 21

A

1	2	3	4	5
escape	oa	wart	greatest	ladies
favorite	toast	warts	gentlemen	change
Alaska	toaster	rough	twisted	tomorrow
remove	moan	pillow	surprise	tadpole
blue	float	suit	welcome	
	soak			

6

large
family
goldfish
sometimes

7

Vocabulary words

1. breeze
2. crowd
3. introduce

B
Aunt Fanny Changes Her Ways Ⓐ

The fleas in Aunt Fanny's Flea Circus were tired of the way Aunt Fanny was treating them. Ⓑ They made up their minds to do something about it. Carl spoke for all the fleas. He went to Aunt Fanny and tried to tell her that she would have to change her ways. But she wouldn't even listen to him. Ⓒ

"Please, Carl," she said. "Can't you see I'm late for dinner? Now be a good little flea and go back to your nice little match box."

Carl was so mad that he kicked a big speck of dust. Ⓓ ❋ 2 ERRORS ❋

"Go to your dinner," he yelled as loud as he could. Things will be different tomorrow."

Aunt Fanny was in for a great big surprise the next day. The circus was packed with people. Aunt Fanny picked up her stick and bowed to the crowd. People clapped. "Ladies and gentlemen," she said. "Welcome to the greatest flea show in the world." She introduced the first act, Martha Jumpjump on the high wire. Ⓔ Aunt Fanny waved her stick and

Martha went up to the high wire. But she didn't skip rope while hopping on one leg. She walked to the middle of the wire and fell off.Ⓕ "Booo," the crowd yelled.Ⓖ

The next act was Henry Ouch. He got in the cage with three rats. But he didn't make the rats do tricks. He hopped around the cage while the rats went to sleep.Ⓗ "Boo," the crowd yelled.Ⓘ

The next act was Carl Goodscratch. He went up to the top of his 48 centimeter ladder. Then he looked up at Aunt Fanny and said, "Don't you think that you should treat us better? Don't you think that you should give us more money and give us a better place to live?"Ⓙ

Aunt Fanny looked at the little flea. Then she looked at the crowd. They looked mad. "Yes, Carl, yes, yes, yes," she said. "Do the dive and I will share with you."Ⓚ

"Do you really mean that?" Carl asked.

"Yes, yes, yes, yes, yes," Aunt Fanny said. Her hand was shaking so much that the stick was making a breeze.Ⓛ

So Carl did a dive. People say it was the best dive he ever did. He twisted around five times. He made seven loops. And he landed in the water without making any splash at all.Ⓜ

The crowd went wild. "Yea, yea," the people cheered. "What a show!" they shouted.Ⓝ

Now everybody in Aunt Fanny's Flea Circus is happy. Aunt Fanny is happy because the fleas work harder and put on a better show. The fleas are happy because they live in a great big cookie box. And they have lots and lots of money.Ⓞ ❄ 9 ERRORS ❄

LESSON 22

A

1	2	3	4
oa	suit	favorite	cover
boast	blue	escape	covered
foam	remove	escaped	floating
road	removed	escaping	sometimes
roast	Alaska		family
float			

5	6	7
goldfish	hundreds	turn
large	toad	return
tadpoles	members	returned
pillow	Toadsville	rough
toaster	thousands	warts

Telling How Two Objects Are the Same

When you tell how two objects are the same, you say the same thing about both objects. Look at object A and object B. Ⓐ

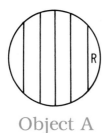

Object A   Object B

Here's one way they are the same: **Both objects have stripes.**

Tell another way they are the same. Ⓑ

C

Martha Jumpjump Takes a Trip Ⓐ

Test yourself on what you've learned.

Martha Jumpjump went on a vacation. Ⓑ She left the circus and jumped and jumped and jumped until she came to something that looked very good to her. It was an animal that was about half a meter long. It was brown and black and white. It had long ears and short hair. Ⓒ That dog was in very good shape because it had just been to a place where it exercised a lot. Ⓓ That dog also changed the way it ate. Ⓔ

"This is for me," Martha Jumpjump said. Ⓕ

❋ 2 ERRORS ❋

With all her legs, she gave a great leap and landed on the animal. Ⓖ

She then started to have a good dinner. Ⓗ But the animal scratched and scratched at her. So Martha jumped off this animal.

Now, she was inside a building. She jumped up and landed on a large desk. Next to her were some flat rulers and one round ruler with marks on its side. Ⓘ Show how far apart those marks were. Ⓙ

Martha jumped down from the desk. Next, she landed on a strange animal with the longest hair you have ever seen. **K**

Martha was not a cat flea and she was not a human flea.**Ⓛ** She was not the kind of flea that liked those strange long-haired animals so she jumped off the moop to find something she liked better.

Soon she found a short-haired animal that was about a meter long.**Ⓜ** Martha jumped onto the animal's tail and began to eat.**Ⓝ** This animal had long ears and liked to hunt.**Ⓞ** Just then another animal came along. This animal was about 1 hundred centimeters long and it had curly hair.**Ⓟ**

Martha was trying to make up her mind about which animal would make the best meal when suddenly a fat man in a red suit came into the room.**Ⓠ** With him was an animal that was about a meter tall at the shoulder and had large, horny things sticking out of its head.**Ⓡ** Martha said to herself, "This place is crazy. I'm going back where I belong." So she did.**Ⓢ**

 9 ERRORS

LESSON 23

A

1	2	3	4
fourth	clearly	toad	pillow
half	smoky	blue	floating
breath	crazy	Alaska	thousands
toward	already	favorite	sometimes
second	stubby	large	Goad
shovel			

5	6	7
toaster	covered	returned
goldfish	Toadsville	members
rough	hundreds	family
escaped	removed	tadpoles
escaping	warts	

B

Facts about Toads and Frogs

Toads and frogs are members of the same family.(A)

Here are facts about toads and frogs:

- They are born in water, and they live in the water until they are full grown.(B)
- At first toads and frogs are tadpoles that have no legs.(C)
- Then tadpoles grow two back legs.(D)
- Then they grow two front legs.(E)
- Then their tails disappear.(F)
- When their legs are big and strong, frogs and toads live on the land.(G)

C

Goad the Toad Ⓐ

Once there was a toad named Goad. Goad was the biggest toad you have ever seen. Goad was bigger than a stone. Goad was bigger than a baseball. Goad was bigger than a toaster.Ⓑ But Goad was not only big. She was smart. She was smarter than a frog. She was smarter than a hound. In fact, she was smarter than a trained seal. Not only was Goad big and smart. Goad was fast. She was faster than a cat chasing a mouse.Ⓒ

Goad lived near a large lake called Four Mile Lake. Ⓓ It was called Four Mile Lake because it was four miles from one end of the lake to the other. ❀ 2 ERRORS ❀

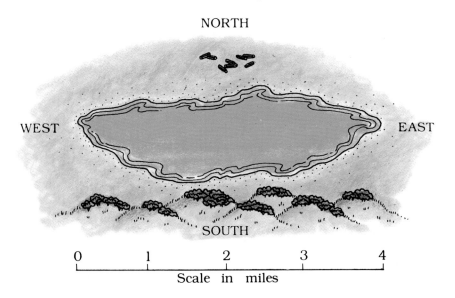

There were a lot of spots on Four Mile Lake that Goad liked to visit. Sometimes, she would hop over to the logs that were near the north shore of the lake.Ⓔ Sometimes, she would hop over the hills on the south shore.Ⓕ Sometimes, she would go for a dip near the east shore of the lake.Ⓖ When Goad was in the water, she was not fast. She could not swim as fast as a seal. She could not swim as fast as a goldfish. In fact, she could not swim as fast as a very slow frog.Ⓗ When Goad was in the water, she looked like a floating pillow with two big eyes.Ⓘ

Because Goad was so big, and so fast, and so smart, thousands of hunters went to Four Mile Lake every year to see if they could catch Goad.Ⓙ People came from the circus. They knew that if they had Goad, they could put on a show that would bring thousands of people to the circus.Ⓚ Hunters came from zoos. They knew that people would come from all over to visit any zoo that had a toad like Goad. Some hunters came because they wanted to become rich.Ⓛ Goad was worth thousands of dollars to anybody who could catch her. But nobody was able to catch her.Ⓜ ❋ 6 ERRORS ❋

LESSON 24

A

1	2	3	4
wild	action	boasted	already
silence	mansion	removed	Toadsville
group	impression	escaped	hundreds
women	motion	Alaska	shovel
swallow	mention	escaping	fourth
tongue			

5	6	7
half	balloon	warts
second	ground	covered
breath	underground	rough
third	crazy	stubby
taste		clearly

8
Vocabulary words
1. escape
2. favorite

B
More Facts about Toads and Frogs

Toads and frogs are members of the same family. But toads are different from frogs. Here are some facts about how they are different:

- Toads have skin that is rough and covered with warts. (A)
- Toads have no teeth. (B)
- The back legs of toads are not as big or strong. (C)

C
Goad Uses Her First Trick (A)

*Goad lived near Four Mile Lake. Down the road from the lake was a town. The name of that town was Toadsville. It was named Toadsville because so many people who visited the town had come to hunt for a big, smart, fast toad. (B) And in the evening you could find hundreds of people sitting around Toadsville talking about Goad. First they would talk about some of the traps that had been made to catch Goad. Then they would tell how Goad escaped. One of their favorite stories is the one of the great big net. (C) ✿ 2 ERRORS ✿

Five hunters from Alaska* had come to Four Mile Lake with a net that was nearly a mile wide. They waited until Goad was on a hill where there were no trees, just some white rocks. Then they flew over the hill in a plane and dropped the great big net over the hill.**❶** Goad was under the net. The five hunters rushed to the place where Goad had last been seen. But there was no Goad. There was some grass and five large white rocks. The hunters removed the net and began to go over every centimeter of the ground. **❷** Suddenly, one of the hunters noticed that the biggest rock was moving. The biggest rock wasn't a rock at all. It was Goad.

She had moved near the other rocks. Then she had turned over on her back so that her white belly was showing. That belly looked like a white rock. Suddenly she turned over. "There she is," one of the hunters yelled, but before the others could turn around, Goad hopped down the side of the hill and was gone.**Ⓕ** 🌸 6 ERRORS 🌸

LESSON 25

A

1	2	3	4
station	roast	mention	boasted
vacation	blue	fourth	motion
session	already	half	breath
lotion	action	impression	third
mission	shovels	second	balloon

5	6	7	8
swallow	tongue	groups	chance
swallowed	silence	tramping	grams
underground	wild	weakness	fifteen
taste	women	problem	toward

9
Vocabulary words
boast

B

How Toads Catch Flies

Toads eat flies. A toad catches flies with its long, long tongue. Ⓐ A toad's tongue is almost as long as the toad. Ⓑ A toad's tongue is covered with sticky goo. The tongue moves so fast that it hits a fly before the fly can move. The fly sticks to the tongue. Ⓒ When the toad pulls its tongue back, the fly comes with it.

The pictures below show a toad's tongue catching a fly. Ⓓ

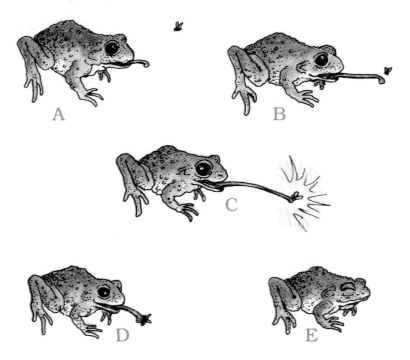

A

B

C

D

E

C

Food Traps Ⓐ

The people in Toadsville like to tell stories about Goad and how she escaped from traps. They tell about how she once escaped from the great big net. Ⓑ The people also tell how Goad got away from food traps. One of the hunters' favorite tricks was to make food traps.

All food traps work the same way. You put out some food that a toad likes. Maybe you put some blue flies on the ground. My, my, how toads love those blue flies. Then you make a trap that closes on the toad when she goes for the food. ❋ 2 ERRORS ❋

We tie a string to one of the blue flies. When that fly is moved, the string moves. Ⓒ The string is tied around a stick. Ⓓ So when the fly moves, the string moves. And when the string moves, the stick moves. Ⓔ That stick holds up a net. So when the fly moves, the string moves. And when the string moves, the stick moves. And when the stick moves, the net falls over the toad. Ⓕ

Look at the picture. It shows a food trap. The arrow on the string shows which way the fly will move when the toad grabs it. Ⓖ When the string moves that way, the stick will move the same way. Ⓗ When the stick falls over, the net will fall down.

If you believe the stories they tell in the town of Toadsville, Goad has escaped from over five hundred food traps. Not all these stories are true. Goad has escaped from four hundred food traps, but that's a lot of escaping for one toad. How did she do it? You already know one of her tricks. Ⓘ You'll find out about more of her tricks in the next story. 🌀 6 ERRORS 🌀

LESSON 26

A

1	2	3	4
either	direction	moan	weakness
grandmother	vacation	young	stubby
arrive	session	wild	problem
interested	nation	women	clearly
	instruction	tramping	chance

5	6	7	8
fifteen	breath	toward	third
grams	shovels	balloon	tongue
groups	half	taste	underground
second	fourth	swallowed	smoky

9
Vocabulary words
1. famous
2. silence
3. impression
4. boast

B

Facts about Moles

Today's story tells something about moles. Here are some facts about moles:

- Moles are animals that spend nearly all their time underground.Ⓐ
- Moles are about the same size as toads.Ⓑ
- Moles cannot see very well.Ⓒ
- Moles have legs like shovels.Ⓓ

C

Balloons

Here's a rule about balloons:

- The bigger the balloon gets, the more light you can see through it.Ⓐ

D

Goad's Four Tricks Ⓐ

Goad has escaped from four hundred food traps. She has four tricks that she uses to escape from those traps. Ⓑ One trick is to make herself look like a rock, the way she did when she escaped from the great net.

Her second trick is to dig. Ⓒ You wouldn't think that a toad the size of a pillow could dig very fast, but you have never seen Goad dig. She can dig so fast that worms get mad at her. Ⓓ She can dig faster than a snake. She can even dig faster than a mole. And moles have legs like shovels. Ⓔ ✿ 2 ERRORS ✿

Goad's third trick is to eat the trap. Ⓕ If the food trap is a big wooden box that drops over Goad, that fat toad just smiles to herself and starts eating. Ⓖ

Her fourth trick is to blow the trap away. Ⓗ That's right. She takes in a big breath of air. When she does this, she gets bigger. Ⓘ She gets so big that you can see right through her. She looks just like a brown and green balloon. Ⓙ When she is nearly two times the size of a pillow, she blows. The wind comes out of her mouth so fast that she can blow most traps a hundred meters away.Ⓚ That's how she got away from the famous steel trap.Ⓛ

A man came from England. The man boasted that he had made a trap that could hold any toad. "No toad can eat through this trap," he said. "And no toad can dig under this trap if I put it on hard rock."

And that's just what he did.Ⓜ He propped up the steel trap next to the road, where there was no dirt, just hard rock. Then he put sixty blue flies under the trap. There is no toad in the world that can stay away from sixty blue flies. So before very long, out popped Goad. Her tongue came out. In one gulp, she had swallowed half of the flies. She was ready for her second gulp, when BONG.Ⓝ

The famous steel trap came down over her. "I told you I could catch her," the man from England boasted as he ran down the road toward the trap. But before he was halfway there, something happened. You could hear the sound of wind. It sounded like air leaking from a tire. Then there was silence. Then there was a great blast of wind, and the famous steel trap went sailing through the air. ⓞ Goad had used her fourth trick. 8 ERRORS

LESSON 27

A

1	2	3	4
course	oi	women	wild
movie	noise	grams	vacation
exact	voice	either	weakness
trouble	point	young	problem
opposite	oil	groups	clearly
engine	coin		

5	6	7	8
fifteen	order	simple	torch
chance	ordering	arrived	torches
grandmother	holler	interested	motioned
bother	action	question	fourteen
	settled		

9
Vocabulary words
1. ordering
2. motion
3. impression

Binoculars

Here is a picture of binoculars:

Follow these instructions:

1. Hold your hands so they make circles. Ⓐ

2. Now look through the circles made by your hands. Ⓑ

Looking through binoculars is like looking through the circles made by your hands. But when you look through binoculars, things look very, very big.Ⓒ Things may look ten times as big as they look without binoculars.

If you see this through the circles made by your hands

you would see this through a strong pair of binoculars.Ⓓ

If you saw something that looked one centimeter tall through the circles made by your hands, that thing would look ten centimeters tall through strong binoculars.

C
The Brown Family
Comes to Catch Goad Ⓐ

Steel traps couldn't catch Goad.Ⓑ Nets couldn't hold her either. Hundreds of men, women, boys, and girls tramping over the hills every summer couldn't catch her. Even trained hunters and trappers failed.Ⓒ But if you listen to the groups of people talking in the town of Toadsville, you know what Goad's only weakness is.Ⓓ She can't swim fast. When she's in the water, she's like a great fat lump, with stubby legs that can hardly push her along.Ⓔ At least a thousand people must have said, "If we could just find her when she's swimming, there's no way she could get away."   ❋ 2 ERRORS ❋

That sounds like an easy thing to do, but there is one problem. You first have to find Goad when she is in the water.Ⓕ

There's an old man in the town of Toadsville who shows pictures of Goad swimming in the lake. The old man took the pictures from high above the lake. Everyone who sees the pictures says the same sort of thing. They say, "If I saw that toad swimming in the lake like that, I'd get in a boat and catch her."

Sometimes in the summer you can count hundreds of people stationed around the lake.**G** They are ready for action.**H** Some of the people have binoculars.**I** They sit hour after hour, looking through the binoculars. Their great hope is that they will see something like the old man saw—Goad swimming around far out from the shore of the lake.

Last summer, a group of wild hunters had the chance that everybody dreams about.**J** They were ready for action when Goad was swimming in the lake.**K** This group of wild hunters came from the same family, the Brown family.**L** The Brown family was made up of fifteen people. They were on vacation, and they decided to spend all their time looking for Goad.

❀ 6 ERRORS ❀

LESSON 28

A

1	2	3	4
backward	oi	grandmother	settled
quiet	join	question	motioned
wrinkle	boil	interested	fourteen
	broil	holler	torches
	moist	mention	smoky
	soil		

5	6	7
stationed	course	exact
arrived	movies	exactly
simple	diving	pointing
bother	engine	smart
trouble	opposite	outsmart

8
Vocabulary words
1. boiled
2. broiled
3. snapshot
4. impression
5. order
6. motion

B

ANIMALS AND FIRE

You're going to read about how animals act when there is a fire. Here is the rule: **When there is a fire, all animals try to get away from the fire.**Ⓐ

The animals are not interested in hunting for food. The animals are not interested in fighting with other animals. Deer don't like wolves, but when a fire is near, wolves and deer may run side by side.Ⓑ They do not fight or bother each other.

C

Smoke and Wind

You're going to read about smoke and wind in today's story. Here's the rule: **The smoke moves in the same direction the wind moves.**Ⓐ

If the wind blows to the north, the smoke moves to the north.

If the wind blows in this direction ➚ , the smoke blows in this direction ➚ .Ⓑ

D

The Browns Make Up a Plan Ⓐ

The grandmother in the Brown family gave the impression that she was very mean. Ⓑ She was always ordering the other Browns around. Ⓒ And the other Browns did a lot of fighting and yelling. But there's one thing you have to say about the Browns. They were the best hunters that ever came to Toadsville. Ⓓ

When fourteen Browns went running down the hill after something that looked like a great toad, it was something to see. Ⓔ And it was something to hear. That mean old grandmother wasn't far away, yelling at everybody. "Come on, Billy," she'd holler. ❋ 2 ERRORS ❋

Then she'd holler some more. "Run faster. Keep up. Don't look down, Doris. Keep your head up." The people on the west side of Four Mile Lake could hear everything she yelled when she was on the east side. Ⓕ

After spending three days running after everything that moved, the Browns settled down. They had a plan. They didn't mention anything about what they were going to do, but everybody knew that they had a plan. People would question them. "What are you going to do?" But the Browns didn't answer these questions. The grandmother would usually say, "Stop asking questions. We've got work to do."

Their plan was simple. First they stationed Browns around the places that Goad liked the most. Everybody knew where these places were. In fact, you can buy little books in the town of Toadsville that show maps of Goad's favorite spots.Ⓖ

The first Brown to spot Goad was Mike. When he saw Goad on a hill near the south shore of the lake, he didn't try to rush down and catch her. Instead, he motioned to the other Browns.Ⓗ When the other Browns arrived, they put their plan into action.Ⓘ

They gave Goad the impression that the hills were on fire.Ⓙ The wind was blowing toward the lake. So fourteen Browns lit big smoky torches.Ⓚ These torches made great clouds of smoke. The smoke rolled down the hills toward Goad, who was resting in the grass after eating one bee and sixteen blue flies. Goad was very smart and when she smelled the smoke, she did just what the Browns hoped she would do.Ⓛ She hopped toward the lake. Slowly, the fourteen Browns moved down the hill. Hop, hop. Goad moved closer to the water. As the Browns moved closer, Goad thought that the fire was coming closer. Hop, hop. Splash.Ⓜ

✿ 8 ERRORS ✿

LESSON 29

A

1	2	3	4
South America	oi	wrinkle	trouble
United States	spoil	wrinkled	course
Mexico	foil	wrist	exactly
Canada	hoist	wrap	noise
	coin	wrong	movies
	toil		

5	6	7
crazy	pointing	joined
snapshots	opposite	quiet
voice	backward	picnic
diving	outsmart	family
engine	outsmarted	families

8

Vocabulary words

1. exact
2. gust
3. moist
4. wade
5. broiled
6. boiled

B

How Air Moves an Object

In the story for today, you'll read about how air can move an object. You've seen it happen with balloons. When you fill them with air and let them go, they fly around until they run out of air.(A)

Here's the rule about how the balloon moves: **The balloon moves the opposite way the air moves.**(B) Touch the dotted arrow in the picture below.(C)

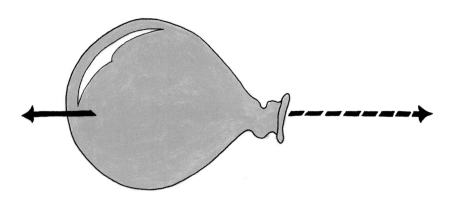

The dotted arrow shows the way the air moves from the balloon.(D)

The balloon moves the opposite way the air moves. The solid arrow shows the way the balloon will fly through the air.(E)

C

Goad in the Water Ⓐ

The Browns had given Goad the impression that a fire was coming down the hill. Ⓑ What really came down the hill was fourteen Browns, each carrying a smoky torch. Ⓒ Goad went into the water, thinking that she was getting away from a fire. But she was doing just what the Browns wanted her to do. Ⓓ Her stubby little legs paddled her out into the lake.

When Goad was about twenty meters from the shore, the grandmother motioned to the Browns, and the Browns came roaring down the hill. Ⓔ ❋ 2 ERRORS ❋

The hills were ringing with noise. Ⓕ Every Brown was yelling, "We've got her." But a much louder voice rang above the others. "Mark, move faster." Ⓖ Of course, it was that grandmother, yelling orders to everybody.

＊It seemed that Goad would never get away from these fourteen screaming Browns. Her little legs were paddling as fast as they could, but she knew that she was in trouble. Browns were racing into the water now, diving, splashing, yelling, coming at Goad like fourteen crazy people. **(H)**

The next part of the story is the part that some people still have trouble believing, because there are still a lot of questions about it. Nobody has movies to show exactly what happened, but a boy from New York who was on vacation took these snapshots that show what happened. **(I)**

The* first snapshot shows the Browns splashing toward Goad. If you look closely at the snapshot, you'll see that Goad looks different. She's getting bigger.Ⓙ That's right. Goad is loading up with air. In the next snapshot, Goad looks bigger. She looks like a balloon with a lot of air in it. She is almost round, with her stubby little legs sticking out in the air.Ⓚ In the same picture, there are three or four Browns reaching out for her. One Brown is diving at her, and he looks like he is only a few meters from her.

In the last snapshot, the Browns are standing in the water, pointing up in the air. In the upper corner of the picture, you can see a little fuzzy mark.Ⓛ That's Goad, flying away from the Browns.Ⓜ ❊ 7 ERRORS ❊

LESSON 30

A

1	2	3
mirror	United States	Canada
record	South America	outsmarted
giant	joined	picnic
earth	quiet	wrinkled
divided	backward	families
country		

4	5	6
Nancy	squeak	stand
spoiled	greet	understand
Mexico	greetings	globe
hurt	pattern	travel
wrong	patterns	traveling

7

Vocabulary words

1. outsmart
2. boiled
3. gust
4. wade
5. broiled
6. moist
7. exact

B

A Big Picnic Ⓐ

The three snapshots of the Browns trying to catch Goad showed Goad getting bigger, Goad getting still bigger, and Goad flying into the air. She had loaded up with air and when the Browns were about to grab her, she unloaded. Ⓑ A great gust of wind came out of her mouth, and she went flying backward. She skipped over the water two times, and then she went straight up into the air. She looked just like a great balloon when you let the air out of it. The Browns just stood there and looked.

 2 ERRORS

One of the Browns said, "Oh nuts," but they seemed to know that Goad had outsmarted them. Ⓒ They didn't run after her. Ⓓ Fourteen Browns stood around in the water watching the great toad land in the weeds about a hundred meters away. Ⓔ Then fourteen soaked Browns waded from the water. They moved slowly.

When they joined the grandmother at the top of the hill, she did something that was very strange. She smiled. Nobody had ever seen her do that before. She had a few missing teeth, but she had a warm smile. It was the kind of old wrinkled smile that makes **you** want to smile. And that's just what happened. When she smiled, one of the little Browns smiled. Then another Brown smiled, and before you knew it, one of the soaking wet Browns began to laugh. Well, before you knew it, they were all laughing. "That's some toad," one of them yelled, and they all laughed harder.Ⓕ

There's something about seeing fifteen Browns laughing and slapping each other on the back. It makes you start laughing too.Ⓖ

A lot of people had gathered to see the Browns try to catch Goad. The first thing you know, the hills were loaded with people who were laughing. Their cheeks were moist because big tears were running down their cheeks.Ⓗ The sound of the laughing was very loud, but pretty soon, a much louder voice rang above the laughing. "Let's have a picnic and forget about that fat old toad."Ⓘ

And that's just what everybody did.Ⓙ All those people with binoculars and nets who had been watching. All the little kids and the families, and the old people, and dogs and cats and pet crows, and fifteen Browns. They all had a picnic. They ate boiled corn and broiled hot dogs.Ⓚ They did a lot of laughing. And some people say that they could hear somebody else laughing. They say that it sounded like a laughing toad.Ⓛ ❋ 9 ERRORS ❋

LESSON 31

A

1	2	3	4
goodbye	South America	country	divided
dollhouse	United States	pattern	earth
outfit	record	countries	giant
doorway	traveling	patterns	Canada
sidewalk	understand	globe	Mexico
peanut			

5	6
mirror	greetings
hurt	squeak
spoiled	wrong
Nancy	shrunk

B

Toads and Warts

Years ago, people thought that this rule was true: **You get a wart where a toad touches you.** Ⓐ

People used to think that you would get a wart on your hand if a toad touched your hand.

C
Telling How Two Things Are Different

Here's how you tell that two things are different. You find something that is not the same about the two things. You tell about the first thing. Then you tell how the second thing is different.

Look at object A and object B. Ⓐ

Object A   **Object B**

Here's one way they are different: **Object A is a square, but object B is not a square.**

You could say it this way: **Object A is a square, but object B is a circle.**

Tell another way that the objects are different. Ⓑ

D
Learning about the World Ⓐ

You will read some stories that tell about traveling to different parts of the world. You must know about the world to understand these stories. Here are facts about the world:

- You live on the world. Ⓑ
- The world is a giant round ball. Ⓒ

- The world is called Earth. Ⓓ
- Most of the world is covered with water. Ⓔ
- Parts of the world are land. Ⓕ

Here is a picture of the world.

Touch a part that is land. Ⓖ
Touch a part that is covered with water. Ⓗ
The land parts of the world are divided into countries.

Parts of the map below are marked with different patterns. ❋ 2 ERRORS ❋

This pattern [ ] shows a country. That country is Canada. Ⓘ

This pattern [ ] shows another country. That country is the United States. Ⓙ

This pattern [ ] shows another country. That country is Mexico. Ⓚ

This pattern [ ] shows all the countries in South America. Ⓛ

Touch the country you live in. Ⓜ

See if you can find different places on a globe.(N)

Your teacher will turn a globe and stop it. Your teacher will call on somebody to find a place. The places on the globe are the same shape as the places on the map above. So take a good look at the shape of these places.(O)

❀ 4 ERRORS ❀

LESSON 32

1	**2**	**3**	**4**
police officer	silly	hurt	squeak
horrible	shiny	mirror	goodbye
heard	tiny	greetings	dollhouse
badge	thirsty	wrong	outfit
edge	Nancy	peanut	
shoe			

5	**6**
doorway	**Vocabulary words**
shrunk	spoiled
scream	
screamed	
record	

B

Telling How Two Things Are Different

Here's how you tell that two things are different. You find something that is not the same about the two things. You tell about the first thing. Then you tell how the second thing is different.

Look at object A and object B.Ⓐ

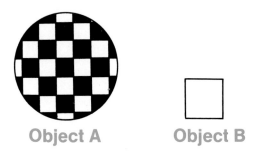

Object A   Object B

Here's one way they are different: **Object A is checked, but object B is not checked.**

You could say it this way: **Object A is checked, but object B is plain.**

Tell another way that the objects are different.Ⓑ

C

Growing Up

In the story you'll read today, a girl doesn't want to grow up. Here are some facts about growing up:

- Humans grow up very slowly.Ⓐ
- Girls grow faster than boys.Ⓑ

- Most girls stop growing taller when they are 15 years old. Ⓒ
- Most boys stop growing taller when they are 18 years old. Ⓓ
- Dogs keep growing until they are one year old. Ⓔ
- Mice keep growing until they are five weeks old. Ⓕ
- Flies do not grow. They are full-grown when they become flies. If you see little flies, they are born little and they die little. Bigger flies are not older. Ⓖ

D

Nancy Wants to Stay Little Ⓐ

Nancy was a spoiled little girl. Ⓑ She liked being little because she could get her way by crying, stamping her feet, turning red in the face, and making lots of noise. When she acted this way, her mother would say, "If you stop crying, I'll give you a treat." Nancy got lots and lots of treats by crying and acting like a little baby girl. Ⓒ

Then one day something happened. Nancy's dad came home from work. He picked her up and said, "How is my big girl?"

※ 2 ERRORS ※

Big girl? Who wants to be a big girl? Nancy knew that if you're a big girl you can't get your way by crying and kicking and stamping and making noise. Ⓓ

After her dad put her down, she went to her room and looked in the mirror. She could see that what her dad said was right. Ⓔ She was getting bigger. The shoes she was wearing were a little tight but when she got these shoes a few months back, they were almost too big for her. Her new striped shirt looked a little small on her. Ⓕ

"Oh nuts," she said in a loud voice. "I don't want to be a big girl." She kicked the mirror and hurt her foot. Then she began to cry and scream and stamp her feet and jump up and down.

That night she had a very bad dream. In her dream she was getting bigger and bigger. When she woke up the next morning she saw something on her bed. It was a record. She rubbed her eyes, picked up the record, and looked at it.

"I do not know how this record got on my bed," she said to herself. "Maybe it is something from Daddy." **G**

She put the record on the record player. A strange voice sang this song:

"If you hate to be tall, tall, tall,

And you want to be small, small, small,

Just say these words in a good loud voice:

Broil, boil, dump that oil." **H**

Nancy played the record two times. Then she said, "That's the worst record in the world." Ⓘ

Later that day she was playing with her friend Sally. Sally was doing tricks that Nancy couldn't do. Sally jumped rope. She played catch with a ball. She did push-ups.

Nancy was getting very mad because she could not do any of those things. Ⓙ At last she said, "Well, I can do something you can't do. I can make myself small by saying some words that you don't know." Ⓚ

"No, you can't make yourself small," Sally said.

"Yes, I can," Nancy said. "But I don't feel like doing it now." Ⓛ

"You don't know any words that could make you small," Sally said.

Nancy said, "Just listen to this." She was very mad. Then in a loud voice she said, "Broil, boil, dump that oil." Ⓜ 🏵 10 ERRORS 🏵

LESSON 33

A

1	**2**	**3**	**4**
piece	climb	police officer	wrong
giant	crumb	heard	squeak
brought	dumb	horrible	boomed
cabinet	thumb	badge	greetings
although		peanut	shiny

5	**6**	**7**
shrunk	silly	cookie
doorway	beyond	edge
outfit	kitchen	shoe
goodbye	wonder	plastic
dollhouse	bathroom	screamed

8
Vocabulary words
1. boom
2. tiny

Facts about Ants

The story you'll read today tells about ants. Here are some facts about ants:

- Ants are insects.
  All insects have six legs.
  So ants have six legs.Ⓐ
- Some ants are red and some ants are black.Ⓑ
- Ants are very strong for their size.Ⓒ

Here's a rule: **An ant can carry an object that weighs ten times as much as the ant.**Ⓓ If an ant weighed as much as an elephant, the ant could carry ten elephants.

- Ants are very light. It would take about one hundred ants to weigh as much as a peanut.

A Green Man Visits NancyⒶ

Nancy had just said some words that she had heard on a record.Ⓑ All at once, the world began to spin around and around.Ⓒ Then Sally started to grow bigger, bigger, and bigger. Sally wasn't the only thing that began to grow. The jump rope that Sally was holding began to get larger.Ⓓ

Sally's voice boomed out, ''Oh, what's wrong? Oh, what's wrong?''Ⓔ The world was still turning and spinning and things were getting larger and larger. Now Nancy was no taller than the grass next to the sidewalk.Ⓕ

Sally was looking down at Nancy. ''Oh, Nancy, what's wrong? You're just a little tiny thing. I'll get somebody to help.'' ❋ 2 ERRORS ❋

Sally dropped her jump rope and ran away.Ⓖ Each step that Sally took shook the ground. Nancy looked around. She was too afraid to cry. And besides, it wouldn't do any good. There was nobody around to treat her like a baby.Ⓗ

An ant came running along the sidewalk. When Nancy looked at the size of the ant, she knew that she had grown even smaller. To her, that ant was the size of a horse,Ⓘ The ant looked very mean—with its round shiny head and six legs running.

Nancy was so frightened that she screamed, but her voice did not sound like it should. Her voice had become smaller as she grew smaller.

Now her voice was so small that it sounded like a little squeak. You couldn't hear her voice five meters away. "Squeak," she screamed. Ⓙ

At that moment, a voice behind her said, "Go away, ant." The ant turned and ran off down the sidewalk. Nancy turned around and saw a little green man no taller than she was. "Greetings," the man said. "I am the one who made the record."

"Hello," Nancy said slowly. Then she said, "Why did you give me that funny record?"

The little man said, "You didn't want anybody to call you a big girl. And you got your wish. Nobody would call a tiny thing like you a big girl." Ⓚ

"I guess you're right," Nancy said. "But I really didn't want to be this little. I'm so little now that . . ." Ⓛ

"Now, now," the green man said. "You should be very, very happy. Even if you grow two times the size you are now, you'll be smaller than a blue fly. Even if you grow twenty times the size you are now, you'll be smaller than a mouse. So you should be very glad."

"Well, I don't . . ." Ⓜ

"I'll walk to your house with you and then I must go," the green man said. "Don't stay outside too long. There are cats and rats and loads of toads that love to eat things your size." Ⓝ ❀ 9 ERRORS ❀

LESSON 34

A

1	**2**	**3**	**4**
decide	police officer	horrible	although
tough	plastic	record	brought
sweater	shoe	cabinet	giant
umbrella	badge	climb	piece
	heard	crumb	pieces

5	**6**	**7**
dollhouse	edge	beyond
outfit	wonder	bedroom
shrunk	cookie	grain
goodbye	bathroom	smooth
doorway	kitchen	

B

Nancy Is Still Tiny Ⓐ

The green man walked with Nancy into her house. Ⓑ They didn't open the door. They walked right through the crack at the bottom of the door.Ⓒ Then Nancy and the green man walked to Nancy's room. As soon as they were inside the room, the green man said, "Goodbye," and he left.

So there was Nancy, all alone in her room. When she had been bigger, she loved to spend time in her room. She had her dolls, her dollhouse, and her toy trains. She had a TV set, and she had records. Things were not the same now that she was so small. ❋ 2 ERRORS ❋

Nancy couldn't play with her dolls because they were at least one hundred times bigger than she was.Ⓓ In fact, the dollhouse was so big that Nancy almost got lost walking around inside it. She tried to turn on her TV, but she couldn't make the button move.Ⓔ That button was five times as big as she was.

Somehow, she made the record player work. It already had a record on it, and when she turned on the player, a great voice came from the player. The voice was so loud that it knocked Nancy down. "If you hate to be tall, tall, tall," the voice boomed. Nancy held her hands over her ears and tried to get away from the horrible noise.Ⓕ It seemed as if a long time passed before the record ended, but suddenly it was quiet in the room again.Ⓖ

Nancy's head hurt and she felt very tired. She went back into the dollhouse and found a bed. The bed was far too big for Nancy but she curled up in a corner of the bed and took a nap.Ⓗ

She slept for about an hour and when she woke up, she heard voices in the room. One voice was her mother's. The other voice belonged to a man who looked bigger than three mountains. He was dressed in a dark blue outfit, and he wore a shiny badge.Ⓘ Nancy's mother was crying.Ⓙ

Nancy's mother said, "I don't know where she went. We've looked all over for her, but nobody's seen her."Ⓚ

The police officer said, "Now, let me make sure I understand this. The last time Nancy was seen she was playing with Sally Allen. Is that right?"Ⓛ

Nancy's mother said, "That's right, she was playing with Sally."

The police officer said, "And Sally Allen

claims that Nancy shrunk up until she was less than one centimeter tall.''

A large tear fell down and almost hit Nancy.Ⓜ The tear was bigger than she was. "I don't know what made Sally make up such a crazy story," Nancy's mother said.Ⓝ "But all I know is that my dear little Nancy is gone and I miss her. I love her very much.''

"Here I am, Mom," Nancy shouted from the doorway of her dollhouse. But her voice was so small that it sounded like a tiny, tiny squeak that wasn't as loud as the sound a new shoe makes when it squeaks.Ⓞ ❀ 10 ERRORS ❀

LESSON 35

1	2	3
plastic	decide	kitchen
umbrella	smooth	bedroom
sweater	bathroom	cookie
tough	grain	beyond

4	5
wonder	brought
edge	although
pieces	crumb
giant	cabinet
	climb

B

Sounds That Objects Make

In lesson 33 you read about Nancy's voice and what happened to it when she became smaller and smaller.Ⓐ

Here's the rule about your voice: **If you get smaller, your voice gets higher.**Ⓑ

Follow these instructions:Ⓒ

1. Place a plastic ruler so that one end of it is on your desk and the other end hangs over the edge of the desk. Make sure that most of the

ruler hangs over the desk. Picture 1 shows how to place the ruler on your desk.Ⓓ

2. Hold down the end of the ruler that is on the desk.

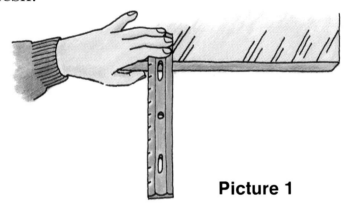

Picture 1

3. Bend the other end of the ruler down. Then let it go so it snaps back. The ruler will make a sound.

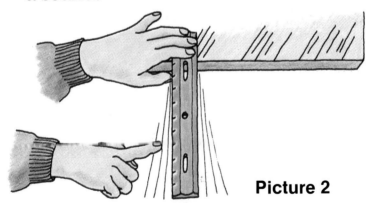

Picture 2

4. Now move the ruler so that less of the ruler hangs over the edge of the desk. The ruler will make a sound that is higher.

5. Now move the ruler so that even less of the ruler hangs over the edge of the desk. The ruler will make a sound that is even higher.Ⓔ

   The ruler works just like your voice. When the part that hangs over the edge gets smaller, the sound gets higher.Ⓕ

C

1	2	3
sink	across	thumb
away	show	cardboard
hurry	dancing	point
pencil	toad	without
grow	around	great
drank	impression	hallway
forest	boast	world
apart	prancer	family
thirsty	direction	sidewalk
flow	arrow	opposite
motioned	noise	gentlemen
another	forward	heard
hungry	voice	quiet
climb	toaster	wrong
shore	action	instruction

LESSON 36

A

1
decide
probably
tough
sweater
umbrella
learn

2
crumb
giant
climb
although

3
cabinet
piece
grain
squirrel

4
wobble
dew
close
closely
wobbled

5
stretch
easy
easily
stretched
smooth

6
scare
scary
ride
stride
bedroom

7
bathroom
wonder
cookie
beyond

8
brought
building
tube
kitchen

9
Vocabulary words
1. catch your breath
2. stale
3. hoist

B

Sugar Shines

The story you'll read today talks about how sugar shines.Ⓐ A grain of sugar is much smaller than an ant. It is no bigger than a grain of sand.Ⓑ

The picture shows what a grain of sugar would look like if it were very big.Ⓒ The grain in the picture has sharp corners. Each side is very smooth. The sugar looks like glass. And the sugar shines like glass.Ⓓ

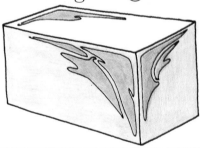

C

Nancy Finds Something to Eat Ⓐ

Nancy was shouting and waving her arms, but her mother and the police officer didn't see her as they walked from the room.Ⓑ Although Nancy ran as fast as her tiny legs could move, she couldn't keep up with them. By the time she reached the doorway to her bedroom, she was tired. For her mother and the police officer, the walk to the doorway took only a few steps. But for Nancy it was a long, long run.Ⓒ

Nancy decided not to follow her mother beyond the bedroom door. Nancy didn't want to get lost.Ⓓ So she stood there trying to catch her breath.Ⓔ ❋ 2 ERRORS ❋

Then she walked slowly back toward her dollhouse. On the way, she looked at all the bits and pieces of things that were stuck in the carpet. Between those giant ropes of blue and green were giant pieces of dirt and giant crumbs.Ⓕ One crumb was the size of a bucket next to Nancy.Ⓖ It was a cookie crumb. "I wonder how long it's been here," Nancy said to herself. "I wonder if it's stale."Ⓗ She felt silly for the thought that was going through her head.Ⓘ She was thinking, "If that cookie crumb is any good, I'll eat the whole thing. It will be like eating the world's biggest cookie."

So she bent over and sniffed the cookie crumb.Ⓙ Then she tapped it with her fist. Then she broke off a little piece. That piece sparkled with shiny sugar.Ⓚ Slowly, she brought the piece of cookie to her mouth and took a tiny bite

from it. "Not bad," she said to herself.Ⓛ "Not bad at all." She took a big bite and another. With two hands she lifted up the whole crumb and began to eat it. She ate about half of it, and then she stopped. She wasn't hungry any more.

"I need a glass of water," she said to herself.Ⓜ She didn't really need a glass of water. She needed much less than a drop of water.Ⓝ But how do you get water when you're smaller than a fly? How do you get water if you don't know how to reach something as high as a kitchen cabinet or a bathroom sink?Ⓞ

"Water," Nancy said to herself. "I must find water."Ⓟ ❀ 8 ERRORS ❀

LESSON 37

A

1	2	3
finally	building	closely
thirsty	probably	wobbled
squirrel	tough	easily
dew	sweater	stretched
	umbrella	scary

4	5	6
weigh	finish	wonder
quick	cover	stride
quickly	discover	wondered
weighs	finished	wondering
learn	discovered	strider

7	8
early	**Vocabulary words**
tube	**1.** lawn
slow	**2.** hoist
slowly	

B

Water Has a Skin

The next story tells about the skin that water has.Ⓐ You can see how that skin works by filling a small tube with water. Here's a picture of what you will see.

- The top of the water is not flat.
- The skin bends up in the middle.Ⓑ

C

Facts about Dew

The story you'll read today talks about dew.Ⓐ The drops of water that you see on grass and cars early in the morning is called dew.Ⓑ

Here are some facts about dew:

- Dew forms at night.Ⓒ
- Dew forms when the air gets cooler.Ⓓ
- Dew disappears in the morning when the air warms up.Ⓔ

D   Nancy Tries to Get Some Water Ⓐ

If Nancy knew more about very small things, she wouldn't have been so afraid of climbing to high places to find water. Here's the rule. **If tiny animals fall from high places, they don't get hurt.** Ⓑ If we dropped an ant from a high airplane, the ant would not be hurt at all when it landed on the ground. A mouse wouldn't be hurt either. Ⓒ A squirrel wouldn't be badly hurt. A beagle would probably be killed. And you can imagine what would happen to an elephant. Ⓓ

Nancy was thirsty, so thirsty that she wanted to yell and scream and stamp her feet like a baby. Ⓔ   ❋ 2 ERRORS ❋

Nancy knew that it wouldn't do any good to act like a baby. So she made up her mind to start thinking. She was pretty smart. She said to herself, "If it were early morning, I could go out and drink dew from the lawn." Ⓕ But the grass was not moist with dew, and Nancy couldn't wait until morning. Ⓖ

So she went to the bathroom, looking for water. She had walked from her bedroom to the bathroom hundreds of times before, but this time it wasn't a walk. It was a long, long trip. She finally arrived in the bathroom. She walked around as she made up a plan for getting water. Here's that plan: She would climb up the corner strip of the cabinet. That strip was made of rough wood and it was easy to grip. It went straight to the top of the cabinet. Ⓗ

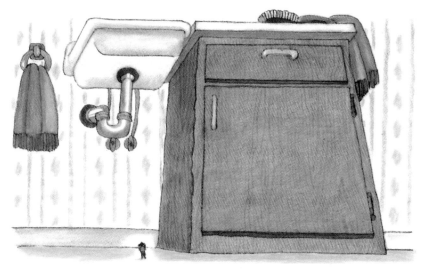

Nancy didn't know what kind of problem would meet her at the top of the cabinet. But first she had to get to the top. So up she went. She hoisted herself up one centimeter, two centimeters. Slowly, up. Then she began moving faster and faster. "This isn't too hard," she said to herself. When she was almost at the top, she reached a spot where the strip was moist with oil. And she slipped. Ⓘ

She fell all the way to the floor. Ⓙ The fall scared her. She landed on her back. For a moment she didn't move. Then she got up slowly, testing her arms and legs to make sure that they weren't hurt. She had fallen from something that was higher than a 1 hundred story building for Nancy, and she wasn't hurt. Ⓚ She wasn't hurt at all, not one broken bone. Not one scratch. Not even an ouch. Ⓛ

"I don't know what's happening," Nancy said to herself. "But I'm not afraid to try climbing that cabinet again."

This time she got to the top. Ⓜ ❊ 9 ERRORS ❊

LESSON 38

A

1
refrigerator
search
complain

2
easily
umbrella
strider
wobbled
closely

3
stretched
tough
scary
sweater
quickly

4
discovered
weighed
finished
cover
weighs

5
learn
wondered
scale
learned
wondering

6
fright
frighten
darkness
slowly
frightened

7
beetle
flies
houseflies
cherry
beetles

B

More about the Skin That Water Has Ⓐ

When we fill a tube with water, you can see that the water has skin. You can use a dish of water and a hair to show that water has a skin. Ⓑ

First you can float a hair on water. If you're careful, the hair won't even get wet. It will just rest on the skin of the water. Ⓒ

Hair A in the picture is resting on the water. Ⓓ

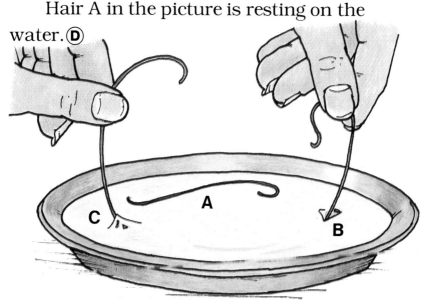

Now hold a hair the way the hands in the picture are holding hair B. Ⓔ

Push the hair down through the skin of the water. As you push down, you can see the skin of the water bending down next to the hair. When the hair goes down, the skin goes down. Hair B is being pushed down.Ⓕ Look at the skin next to it.Ⓖ

Now slowly pull the hair up. When it moves up, you can see the skin hanging onto the hair. When the hair goes up, the skin goes up.Ⓗ Hair C is moving up.Ⓘ

C

Nancy Gets Some WaterⒶ

Nancy had climbed to the top of the cabinet. She was ready to have a nice drink of water. Next to the sink there were lots of drops of water. Some drops were bigger than she was. Some drops were about the size of an open umbrella top.Ⓑ She rushed over to them.

Nancy didn't know much about water drops. Here's the rule: **Water drops have a skin that goes all the way around them.**Ⓒ That skin is tough. If you are at a pond, you may see little insects called water striders that walk right on the top of the water. ❋ 2 ERRORS ❋

If you look closely, you can see that the legs of water striders make little dents in the water but their legs do not go into the water. The legs just bend the skin of the water without going through the skin. Ⓓ

Nancy had seen water striders, but she didn't think about how tough the skin of water must be if you are very small. She ran over to one drop of water. The drop of water came up to her knees. Then she bent over and touched the water drop with her hands. It felt like a water balloon. Ⓔ When she pushed, the skin moved in. But her hand didn't go through the skin.

"How do insects drink water?" she thought for an instant. Then she got back to her problem. "How am I going to drink?" Ⓕ

"I'll just hit it harder," she thought. She made a fist, wound up and swung as hard as she could swing. Her fist went right through the skin of the drop.**(G)** Her hand was wet and her arm was wet. She pulled her hand back, but it didn't come out easily. It stuck at the wrist.**(H)**

She pulled and tugged, and the skin of the water stretched out. Finally, **pop.(I)** Her hand came out, and the skin of the water drop wobbled back into its round shape.**(J)**

Nancy thought about the best way of getting water from the drop. At last, she backed up a few steps, put her head down, and charged the drop of water. Her head hit the water drop and **pop.** Her head went through the skin.**(K)** She drank quickly, trying not to get water in her nose. Then she pulled her head back.**(L)** The skin of the water tugged at her neck. The water pulled at her neck the way a tight sweater pulls on your neck when you try to take it off.**(M)** Nancy pulled hard, and **pop.** Her head came out of the drop.

"That was scary," she said out loud.**(N)**

※ 9 ERRORS ※

LESSON 39

A

1	2	3	4
decision	weighed	cherry	learned
regular	discovered	houseflies	complain
instead	weighs	scale	darkness
whole	cover	beetles	complained
manage	wondered		

5	6	7
finished	reply	**Vocabulary words**
refrigerator	replied	1. stale
search	whirl	2. hoist
frightened	swirl	3. lawn
	thirty	

B

Grams

In some stories, you've read about things that do not weigh very much. When we weigh very small things, we use grams. Ⓐ

Here's a rule about grams: **All grams are the same weight.** Ⓑ

If you had a block of water that was one centimeter on all sides, that block would weigh one gram. Ⓒ

A pencil weighs more than a gram. A long pencil weighs about five grams. A short pencil weighs about two grams. Ⓓ

C Comparing Things

When you compare two things, you tell how the things are the same. Then you tell how they are different. Ⓐ When you tell how they are different, you use the word **but.** Ⓑ

Look at object A and object B. Ⓒ When you compare object A and object B, first you tell a way they are the same: **They're both circles.** Then you tell a way they are different: **Object A is big, but object B is not big.** Ⓓ

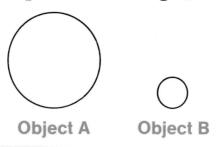

Object A   Object B

Compare object C and object D. First tell a way they are the same. Then tell a way they are different.Ⓔ

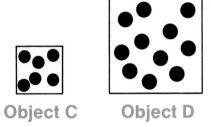

Object C   Object D

Compare object E and object F. First tell a way they are the same. Then tell a way they are different.Ⓕ

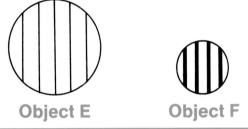

Object E   Object F

D

Nancy Is Hungry AgainⒶ

Nancy found out three things about being very small.Ⓑ She found out that small things have very high voices. She also discovered that very small things do not hurt themselves when they fall from high places. The third thing she discovered was that a drop of water is very different to someone who is quite small.Ⓒ

During her first night of being small, Nancy found out a fourth fact about being small. Here's the rule: **The food that very small animals eat each day may weigh as much as the animal.** Ⓓ ❉ 2 ERRORS ❉

Let's say a small animal weighs one gram. Ⓔ The food that the animal eats each day may weigh one gram. The food that bigger animals eat each day does not weigh as much as the animals. Ⓕ An elephant may eat two hundred pounds of food each day, but the elephant weighs much more than two hundred pounds. An adult human may eat five pounds of food each day, but the adult weighs much more than five pounds. A large pointer may eat three pounds of food every day but the pointer weighs much more than three pounds.

Nancy learned this rule during the first night that she was very small. Ⓖ She woke up in the middle of the night. She was very hungry. So she got up from her dollhouse bed and went looking for another chunk of cookie that was on her rug. She found one and ate it. Then she felt thirsty, so she went back to the bathroom, climbed to the top of the cabinet, and drank from a drop of water.

"That's scary," she said when she finished.**H**

She went back to bed in her dollhouse, but before the sun came up, she woke up again.**I** She was hungry. The cookie crumbs were gone so she couldn't eat cookie crumbs. She tried to forget about how hungry she was. Here's what she said to herself, "Nancy, you've already eaten a chunk of cookie that weighs almost as much as you weigh." Then she wondered, "How can I still be hungry?"

The feeling of hunger did not go away. After a few minutes, she got out of bed. "Oh nuts," she said. "I'm going to have to go hunting for food."**J** ❋ 8 ERRORS ❋

LESSON 40

A

1	2	3
scale	manage	whirl
beetles	whole	replied
cherry	instead	search
houseflies	regular	swirl
	decision	

4

frightened
refrigerator
darkness
complained
thirty

B

More about Grams

You learned about grams. You know that grams are used to weigh some kinds of things.Ⓐ

You know how much water it takes to weigh one gram.Ⓑ You know how much a long

pencil weighs.**©** You know how much a short
pencil weighs.**©**

Here are some facts about how much other
things weigh. A cherry weighs about ten
grams.**©** An apple weighs about two hundred
grams.**©**

Most insects weigh much less than a gram.
Even a very big spider like the spider in the
picture weighs less than a gram.**©**

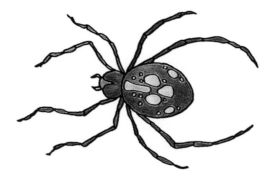

It would take about one hundred ants to
weigh one gram.**⊕**

It would take about thirty houseflies to weigh one gram.Ⓘ

It would take about two hundred fleas from Russia to weigh one gram.Ⓙ

The picture below shows how much some big beetles weigh. How many grams are on the scale?Ⓚ So how much weight is on the side of the scale with the beetles?Ⓛ

C

1	2	3
goodbye	thumb	stretched
silly	mention	discover
dew	boasted	frighten
climb	easily	weighed
spoiled	kitchen	cherry
closely	strider	beetle
shiny	finally	cabinet
giant	station	houseflies
crumb	tough	bedroom
smooth	quickly	wondering
dollhouse	learn	beyond
although	finished	building
hoist	impression	squirrel
piece	wobbled	probably
tiny	scary	decide

LESSON 41

1

expression
prove
worry
remind
couple
important

2

search
complained
darkness
wondering
regular

3

refrigerator
whirl
replied
frightened
swirl

4

instead
manage
darling
managed

5

repeat
whole
either
neither
repeated

6

Vocabulary words
make a decision

B

Nancy Finds Some More Food ⓐ

Nancy went toward the kitchen. ⓑ The
walk seemed to take forever. The house was

dark and Nancy couldn't see well, so she felt the walls and walked slowly toward the kitchen. When she was in the dining room, she could hear the sound of the refrigerator. In fact, she could feel the refrigerator. It shook the floor.

Finally, Nancy reached the kitchen. By now, she was so hungry that she wanted to scream and cry and kick and roll around on the floor like a baby.Ⓒ But she didn't do any of those things because she knew that acting like a baby wouldn't do any good. So she opened her eyes wide and tried to look for scraps of food.

 2 ERRORS

Near the refrigerator, she found something. She bent over and sniffed it. She wasn't sure what it was, but it smelled bad. "I'm not that hungry," she said. "I'll bet that chunk of food has been on the floor for a week."

Nancy walked nearly all the way around the kitchen, but she couldn't find any other food. "I'll bet there's food on the counter," she said to herself.Ⓓ

Up she went, without feeling frightened.Ⓔ She reached the top and began to search the counter top.

She smelled it before she saw it—toast.**(F)** She followed her nose.**(G)** In the darkness, she could just see the toast.**(H)** Three pieces of toast were piled on a plate. To Nancy, the pile of toast looked like a giant ten-story building.**(I)**

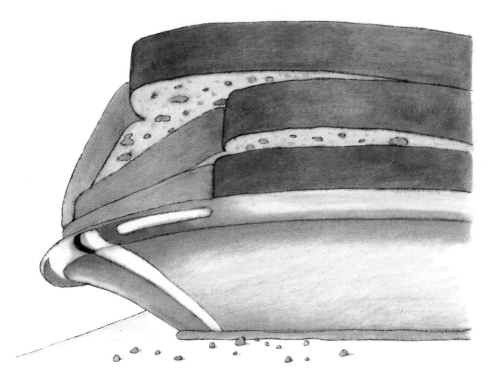

Nancy was wondering how to climb onto the plate so that she could reach the toast. But when she started to walk around the plate, she found crumbs all over the counter.Ⓙ There were crumbs that seemed as big as baseballs and crumbs as big as footballs. There was even one crumb that was the size of a chair.

Nancy picked up a crumb that was the size of a football.Ⓚ She ate it with a loud, "Chomp, chomp, chomp."Ⓛ

When Nancy had been full-sized, she hated toast. She complained when her mother served it. "Oh, not that stuff," she used to say. "I hate toast."

Now that she was small and hungry all the time, she didn't hate toast.Ⓜ In fact, that crumb of toast tasted so good that she ate another piece the size of a football.

Nancy weighed much less than a gram.Ⓝ In one day, she had eaten food that weighed almost a gram.Ⓞ ❋ 8 ERRORS ❋

LESSON 42

A

1
actually
cabbage
maggot
together

2
space
bounce
peace
city
race

3
replied
decision
instead
whirl

4
regular
swirl
darling
repeated
neither

5
worried
important
expression
whole
couple

6
managed
remind
young
youngster
reminds

7
crawl
wiggle
crawled
wiggled

8
Vocabulary words
1. sleep soundly
2. prove
3. make a decision

B THE GREEN MAN VISITS NANCY AGAIN Ⓐ

Nancy was full.Ⓑ She didn't feel like climbing down from the counter top, so she just jumped.Ⓒ For Nancy, it was like jumping from the top of a building that is more than one hundred stories tall. But she landed on her feet as easily as you would if you jumped from a chair to the floor.Ⓓ

She walked back to her dollhouse. By the time she got back in bed, it was almost time for the sun to come up. She wasn't very tired, but she made a decision to sleep.Ⓔ She closed her eyes, and in a few moments, she was sleeping soundly.Ⓕ ❋ 2 ERRORS ❋

"Wake up, wake up," a loud voice said. Nancy opened her eyes. For a moment she didn't know where she was or what was standing in front of her. It was green and it was speaking in a loud voice, "Come on and wake up. Wake up."Ⓖ

"I'm awake," Nancy said. Her voice sounded thick and sleepy. The room was light. In fact, things looked so bright that Nancy had to cover her eyes.Ⓗ "Is that you?" she asked.

The little green man answered, "Of course, it's me. I've come to see if you're happy." ①

"No, I'm not happy," Nancy said.

"And why not?" the green man asked.

"Because I don't like being so little."

"Oh," the green man said and sat down. "I thought you never wanted to get big."

"I was wrong," Nancy replied. "I want to get big. I want to grow up. I want to be back with my mother and my friends."

The little green man said, "I can change you back to your regular size if I want to. But I'm not going to change you unless you tell me some things that you learned." The green man stood up and stared at Nancy. "What have you learned about kicking and screaming and acting like a baby?"Ⓙ

Nancy smiled. "It won't do you any good when nobody is around to treat you like a baby."

The man said, "And when nobody is around, what do you do instead of kicking and crying?"

Nancy said, "You have to take care of yourself."

"Good," the green man said. "I'm glad that you learned things about yourself. But have you learned things about the world you live in?"Ⓚ

"Lots of things," Nancy said, and she began to list them. "I've learned that little things don't hurt themselves when they fall from high places. I've learned that . . ." Suddenly everything seemed to whirl and swirl around. Nancy tried to keep talking. "I've learned . . ." She felt very dizzy.Ⓛ ❀ 9 ERRORS ❀

LESSON 43

1	2	3	4
Kennedy	repeated	race	bounce
busy	darling	thrown	between
taxi	neither	cabbage	actually
realize	space	racing	flies
meant	youngster	maggots	bounced
bullet			

5	6	7	8
wiggled	city	important	block
farther	together	worried	dock
peace	lifetime	expression	whole
peaceful	cities	managed	body
crawled	reminds	couple	

9

Vocabulary words

1. manage

2. prove

B

Facts about Miles

The story in this lesson will tell about miles. Here are some facts about miles.

- We use miles to tell how far it is between places that are far apart.Ⓐ
- Every mile is the same size.Ⓑ
- Every mile is about 16 hundred meters long.Ⓒ

Look at the map. The numbers on the arrows tell how many miles it is from one place to another place.Ⓓ

Touch the arrow that goes from the forest to the hill.Ⓔ The number on the arrow is 3, so it is 3 miles from the forest to the hill.Ⓕ

Touch the arrow that goes from the hill to the lake.Ⓖ

How far is it from the hill to the lake?Ⓗ

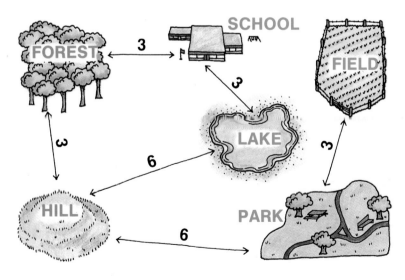

C

Nancy Becomes Regular Size Ⓐ

The whole room seemed to be turning and swirling. Nancy felt so dizzy that she was afraid she would fall over. She kept trying to tell the little green man about the things she had learned. Finally, she managed to say, "I learned that water has a skin."

Nancy closed her eyes and talked very loudly. She hoped that she could stop the dizzy feeling by talking loudly. "And I learned that every day little animals eat food that weighs as much as they do."

Nancy opened her eyes. But she didn't see the little green man. She saw the face of a woman. Ⓑ ❋ 2 ERRORS ❋

The expression on that woman's face was one of shock. Her eyes were wide open and so was her mouth. Ⓒ "Where . . . ," the woman said, "where have you been?"

The expression changed. Tears began to form in the woman's eyes. Then Nancy's mother threw her arms around Nancy. "Oh, Nancy," she said. Her voice was sobbing, and she was holding Nancy very tightly. "Oh, darling," she said. "We've been so worried . . ." **(D)**

Nancy started to cry. She didn't want to cry, but she was so glad to see her mother, and it felt so good to have her mother hold her. She couldn't hold back the tears. "Oh, mother," she said.(E)

For a few minutes, neither Nancy nor her mother said anything.(F) Then, her mother grabbed Nancy's hands and held them tightly as she said, "Nancy, where have you been? The police have been looking for you and . . . And Sally told a crazy story about you becoming very small."(G)

"It's true," Nancy said. "I know it sounds crazy, but I can prove to you that it really happened. I can tell you where the crumbs of toast are on the counter. I can tell you about the drops of water in the bathroom."(H) Nancy said, "And I can tell you other things."(I)

Nancy's mother was smiling and crying and laughing at the same time. "Oh, Nancy, I don't know what to believe, but I'm very glad to have my darling little baby back."(J)

Nancy said, "I'm not a baby. That's the most important thing I learned when I was less than one centimeter tall. I can take care of myself. And I don't mind growing up at all.''

That story took place a couple of years ago. Nancy is still growing up. And she's doing a fine job. She doesn't act like a baby—not even when things go wrong. Instead, she reminds herself, ''I can take care of myself.'' And that's just what she does.(K) 9 ERRORS

LESSON 44

A

1	2	3
bullet	block	city
dock	gun	meant
crawled	Kennedy	busy
bullets	realize	cities
	guns	taxi

4
Vocabulary words
direction

More Facts about Miles

Here are some more facts about miles.

- If you flew from the east side of the United States to the west side of the United States, you would go about 25 hundred miles. Ⓐ
- If you flew from the north side of the United States to the south side of the United States, you would go about 13 hundred miles. Ⓑ

The map shows the United States. Ⓒ

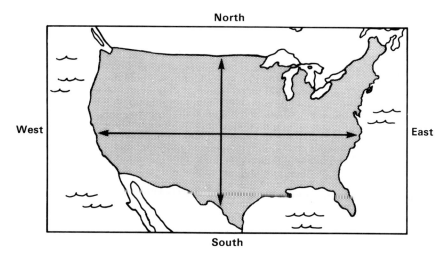

Touch the arrow that goes from the east side to the west side of the United States. Ⓓ

Touch the arrow that goes from the north side to the south side of the United States. Ⓔ

C
A Push in the Opposite Direction Ⓐ

Here's a new rule: **When something moves in one direction, there is a push in the opposite direction.** Ⓑ

You have already seen how this rule works. Look at the picture of Goad. The air is coming out of Goad's mouth in this direction ↘ . Ⓒ So Goad will be pushed in the opposite direction ↖ .

A

If the air came out of Goad in this direction ↙ in which direction would Goad move? Ⓓ
If the air came out of Goad in this direction ⟶ which direction would Goad move? Ⓔ
Look at the picture of the balloon. Show

which way the air is coming out of the balloon. Ⓕ ✿ 2 ERRORS ✿

Now show which way the balloon will be pushed. Ⓖ

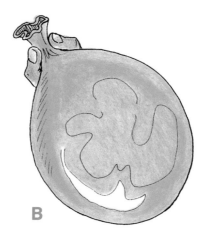

B

*Look at the picture of Goad moving through the air, and see if you can figure out which way the air is coming out of Goad. Ⓗ

C

The pictures below show that there is always a push in the opposite direction. The boy wants to move in this direction ⟶ .Ⓘ The boy can't move in that direction unless there is a push in the opposite direction.Ⓙ

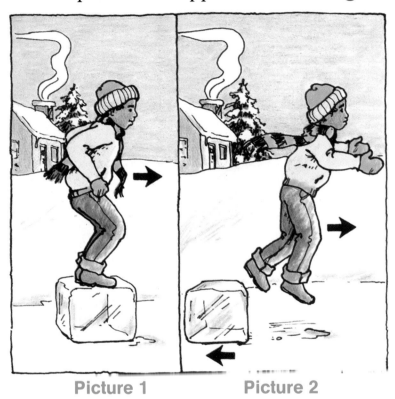

Picture 1   Picture 2

Picture 2 shows that there is a push in the opposite direction. The boy tried to move this way ⟶ . There was a push in the opposite direction. That push made the block of ice slide this* way ⟵ .Ⓚ

Look at the picture of the girl in the boat. She wants to jump from the boat to the dock. Show which direction she will jump. Ⓛ

Picture 3

If she jumps in that direction, there will be a push. Show the direction of the push. Ⓜ

If the rule is right, the girl will try to jump this way ⟵ but the boat will move in the opposite direction. It will move this way ⟶ .

Picture 4 shows what happened when the girl tried to jump to the dock. In which direction did the girl start to move?  **(N)**

Picture 4

In which direction did the boat move? **(O)**
Did the girl land on the dock? **(P)**
The rule about how things move works for everything. When something moves in one direction, there is a push in the opposite direction. **(Q)** 🏵 7 ERRORS 🏵

LESSON 45

1	2	3
bullets	umbrella	replied
guns	regular	youngster
refrigerator	expression	repeated
decision	important	manage
probably		sweater

4	5	6
remind	instead	building
seven	cabinet	weighs
couple	stretched	brought
search	beyond	discovered
although	finally	early

7

wondering
frightened
darkness
houseflies
complained

More about Pushes in the Opposite Direction Ⓐ

In the last lesson you learned an important rule about how things move. You learned that when something moves in one direction, there is always another push. Ⓑ

Bullets from guns move because there is a push in the opposite direction. Jet planes move because there is a push in the opposite direction. Ⓒ

Here's how a bullet works.

Picture 1 shows the direction that the bullet will go. Ⓓ

Picture 1

If the bullet moves in that direction, there must be a push in the opposite direction. Ⓔ

❋ 2 ERRORS ❋

Picture 2 shows what happens when the woman fires the gun. The bullet goes forward. And there is a strong push in the opposite direction. The gun jumps backward, and it pushes backward against the woman. Ⓕ

Picture 2

The picture of a jet engine shows how jet engines work.

The engine is on the wing of the plane. The plane moves forward. Ⓖ If the plane moves forward there has to be a push in the opposite direction.**Ⓗ**

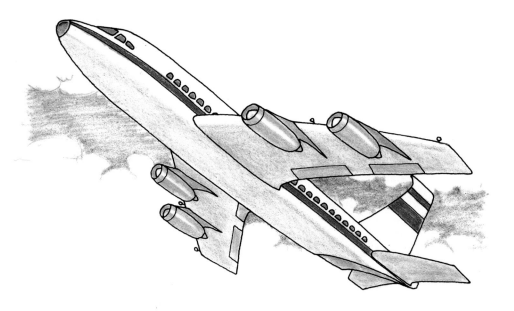

The jet engine shoots air toward the back of the plane very fast.**Ⓘ** The engine works the same way Goad works when she lets air out. The air flies out of the jet engine. There is a push in the opposite direction. So the plane moves forward.**Ⓙ** ❋ 4 ERRORS ❋

LESSON 46

A

1
passenger
San Francisco
flight attendant
speedometer

2
lifetime
actually
bright
brightly
seven

3
purse
chewing
sunlight
jumbo
airport

4
realize
traffic
taxicab
realized
busy

5
Kennedy
meant
belonged
maggots

6
flies
youngster
cabbage
thrown

7
body
together
between
farther
crawled

8
Vocabulary words
realize

B MILES PER HOUR

When we talk about **miles per hour,** we tell **how fast something is moving.** Ⓐ If something goes five miles per hour, it goes five miles every hour. If something goes ten miles per hour, it goes ten miles every hour. Ten miles per hour is faster than five miles per hour. Ⓑ

Which is moving faster, something that goes four miles per hour or something that goes two miles per hour? Ⓒ

Which is moving faster, a boat that goes 20 miles per hour or a boat that goes 23 miles per hour? Ⓓ

Look at the picture below. The numbers below each dog show how fast that dog is running.

How fast is dog A running? Ⓔ
How fast is dog B running? Ⓕ
How fast is dog C running? Ⓖ
Which dog is running fastest? Ⓗ

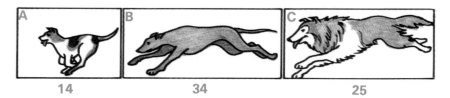

A   14

B   34

C   25

C

Herman the Fly Ⓐ

Herman was a fly. He was born on some old cabbage leaves that had been thrown out. Herman's mother laid eggs on the leaves, and two days after she laid them, Herman was born. Ⓑ He had brothers and sisters. In fact, he had 80 brothers and 90 sisters. All Herman's brothers and sisters were born on those rotten cabbage leaves.

When Herman was a youngster, he didn't look like he did when he was a full-grown fly. When Herman was a youngster, he looked like a worm because he was a worm. Here's the fact: **When flies are born, they are worms called maggots.** Ⓒ ✺ 2 ERRORS ✺

For nine days, Herman was a maggot that crawled around on the cabbage eating and eating and eating. Ⓓ Then Herman felt sleepy. He stopped eating and went to sleep. When he woke up, he had changed. He was a fly. He wiggled out of his old maggot skin, and there he was, a fly. He was one centimeter long. Ⓔ Like all flies, he had six legs and two big eyes.

Here is something that you may not know about flies. Flies do not change size on the outside. But they change size on the inside. Ⓕ When Herman first became a fly, he looked just as big as when he was an old, old fly. But if you looked inside Herman, you would have seen that his outside body was like a shell. Inside that shell is the part of the fly that grows. Ⓖ At first, the inside part is small. It looks like a little tiny foot in a great big shoe. There is lots of

A   B

space between the part that grows and the shell. As the fly gets older and older, the inside part gets bigger and bigger until it fills up the shell.Ⓗ

Anyhow, it didn't take Herman long to grow up. Within nine days he was full-grown and doing those things that flies like to do.Ⓘ He buzzed around. He ate. He loved to find things that were rotten and warm. He rubbed his two front feet together as he rested.

Herman may seem like any other fly to you. But he was different, very different. Herman has the record of flying farther and faster than any fly that has ever lived.Ⓙ Most flies fly a few hundred miles in their lifetimes. A few flies will fly over a thousand miles. Herman flew thousands and thousands of miles. In the next story, you'll find out how he did that.Ⓚ

 8 ERRORS

LESSON 47

1

engine
above
temperature

2

flew
blew
brew
chew
crew

3

airport
sunlight
runway
downtown

4

flight attendant
meant
jumbo
brightly

5

purse
chewing
San Francisco
Kennedy

6

busy
traffic
member
belonged

7

passenger
move
passengers
moving

8

taxicab
believe
above
believing

9

Vocabulary words

1. realized
2. speedometer

Speedometers

You know that **miles per hour** tells **how fast something is moving.** The faster something is moving, the more miles per hour it goes.

Which is moving faster, something that goes five miles per hour or something that goes four miles per hour?Ⓐ

Picture 1 shows a speedometer inside a car that is moving. The arrow is pointing to the number 35. That tells how fast the car is going. How fast is it going?Ⓑ

Picture 1

Picture 2 shows a speedometer inside a car that is not moving. That car is going zero miles per hour.Ⓒ

Picture 2

Look at the speedometers in Picture 3. How fast is car A moving?Ⓓ

How fast is car B moving?Ⓔ

Which car is not moving?Ⓕ

A

B

C

Picture 3

C

Herman Goes to Kennedy Airport Ⓐ

Herman became the fly that flew farther than any other fly. If you want to understand how this happened, you have to know where Herman lived.

Herman was born in New York City. Ⓑ He was born on a cabbage leaf that was about five miles from a large airport called Kennedy Airport. Ⓒ Kennedy Airport is very busy. You can go to Kennedy Airport at any time of the day or night and see planes. Some are in the sky, getting ready to land. Others are on the ground, getting ready to take off.

❋ 2 ERRORS ❋

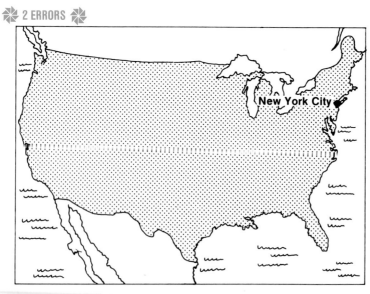

New York City

Herman went to Kennedy airport. Five miles is pretty far for a fly to travel, but Herman didn't fly all the way. He was buzzing around, looking for food, when he saw a nice, warm yellow.Ⓓ He didn't know what it was, but it was warm and yellow. So he landed on it.Ⓔ

It was a brand new taxicab that was on its way to the airport. It was stopped at a traffic light when Herman landed on the roof. When the cab began to move, Herman thought he would fly away, but then he realized that the wind was blowing too fast. Here's the rule: **The faster the cab moves, the faster the wind blows on Herman.**Ⓕ Flies don't take off when

the wind is blowing very fast.Ⓖ Flies use their six legs to hang on as hard as they can. So Herman hung on as hard as he could, and the wind blew and blew.Ⓗ But soon the wind blew slower and slower.Ⓘ And then the wind stopped.Ⓙ The cab had stopped at the airport. For Herman, this stop meant that he could fly away from the cab. For the two women inside the cab, this stop meant that they would have to start working.Ⓚ The women were part of the crew of a jumbo jet.Ⓛ

One woman opened her purse. She took out some money to pay the cab driver. The sun was shining brightly on the things in her opened purse. There was a pack of chewing gum. And there was some candy. CANDY. If there is one thing that flies love more than cabbage leaves and rotten meat, it is candy.Ⓜ And in the warm sunlight, what could be better than a piece of candy that is two times bigger than you are?Ⓝ Herman saw that piece of candy. He made two circles in the air and one S-shaped move.Ⓞ And he landed right on the candy. But just as he was ready to start eating, everything got dark.Ⓟ

✿ 9 ERRORS ✿

LESSON 48

A

1
Chicago
captain
Michigan
heaven
degree
ocean

2
flight attendant
idea
cities
San Francisco
belonged

3
believing
member
passengers
peaceful

4
bounding
downtown
moving
bounced

5
runway
brew
perfect
galley
brewing

6
Denver
metal
shrimp
panel
temperature

7
Vocabulary words
passenger

Airplane Crew Members

Here's a picture of some airplane crew members.

A   B   C   D

A is the pilot. **B** is a flight attendant. What is **C**? Ⓐ On a large jumbo jet, there may be fifteen flight attendants.

Here are the rules:

- The pilot and some other crew members work in the front of the plane. They fly the plane. Ⓑ
- The flight attendants work in the back of the plane. They serve the passengers. Ⓒ

C
Facts about Speed

Here are facts about speed:(A)
- A fast man can run this fast: 20 miles per hour.(B)
- A pointer can run this fast: 35 miles per hour.(C)
- A racing car can go this fast: 2 hundred miles per hour.(D)
- A jet flies this fast: 5 hundred miles per hour.(E)

D
Herman Ends Up on a Jumbo Jet (A)

For the next part of Herman's story, you have to know something about the United States.(B) Kennedy Airport is in New York City. And New York City is on the east side of the United States.(C) Touch New York City on the map.(D)

There are cities on the west side of the United States. One of them is San Francisco.(E) Touch San Francisco on the map.(F)

Herman was in a purse. That purse belonged to a member of a jumbo-jet crew. The

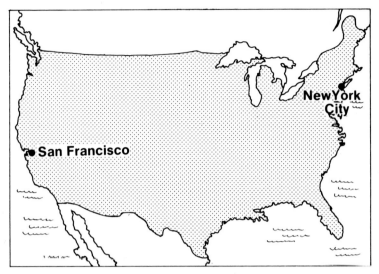

woman had closed the purse, and Herman couldn't get out. ❋ 2 ERRORS ❋

At first, Herman didn't like the idea of being inside a dark place, but then he thought he would try to have a good time anyhow.Ⓖ So he started to eat the candy. Eating it was a little hard because things kept bouncing up and down and up and down.Ⓗ The crew members were walking through the airport on their way to their jumbo jet.

That jumbo jet was going to fly from New York City all the way to San Francisco. Touch the map and show where the jet starts out and where it will land.Ⓘ The trip from New York City to San Francisco is about 25 hundred miles.Ⓙ

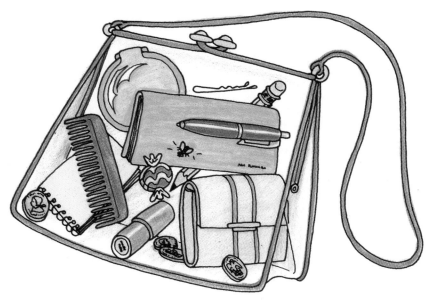

Herman kept trying to eat as the purse
bounced up and down. Then suddenly
everything went this way and that way. The
crew member had tossed her purse on a shelf
inside the jumbo jet. Herman didn't like to be
tossed around like that. "Let me out of this
dark," he thought to himself and tried to fly out
of the purse. Ⓚ

He bounced around for a while, and then
his eyes saw a crack where light was coming in.
Herman ran up the inside of the purse and went
through the crack. There were smells in the air
but most of them did not smell very good to
Herman. They were the clean smells of clean

seats and clean floors and clean windows. Ⓛ

Herman took off to find some better smells
or some better light. Ⓜ He found a nice warm
red. It was fuzzy and very warm. Ⓝ Herman
took a nap. He was on the back of a seat, right
next to the window. The sun was shining
through the window. That felt great. Ⓞ

Suddenly, things were coming after
Herman. A big dark dropped next to him.
"You're not going to get me," Herman thought
and took off. Then something came right toward
Herman. With a little W-shaped move, he got
out of the way. Ⓟ

Here's what had happened. The passengers
had begun to get on the plane. One of them
dropped a coat on the seat back, right next to
Herman. Herman took off and flew in the face of
another passenger. That passenger tried to
brush him away with her hand. Ⓠ

Now Herman could not find a peaceful
place. In every place he landed, somebody
swung at him or tried to brush him away. There
were over three hundred people on this jumbo
jet now, and it was getting ready to take off. Ⓡ

 10 ERRORS

LESSON 49

A

1	2	3	4
passenger	moving	believing	heaven
engine	above	perfect	Chicago
dodge	racing	shrimp	metal
huge	downtown	Michigan	captain
gentle	ocean	galley	couple

5	6	7
face	happen	**Vocabulary words**
Denver	degrees	**1.** heart pounds
panel	temperature	**2.** nose
facing	degree	**3.** runway
brew	happened	

B

Temperature

When we talk about how hot or cold something is, we tell about the **temperature** of the thing.Ⓐ

Something that is very hot has a high temperature.

Something that is very cold has a low temperature. Ⓑ

Is the temperature of ice high or low? Ⓒ

Is the temperature of boiling water high or low? Ⓓ Here's the rule: **When an object gets hotter, the temperature goes up.** Ⓔ

Object A gets hotter. So what do you know about the temperature of object A? Ⓕ

When a floor gets cold, which way does the temperature go? Ⓖ

A glass of water gets hotter. Tell about the temperature. Ⓗ

C

Herman Takes Off for San Francisco Ⓐ

The jet engines on a jumbo jet work the same way that Goad works when she wants to move very fast. When Goad wanted to get away from the Brown family, she let the air rush out. The air rushed out one way, and Goad went flying the other way. That's just how jet engines work. The air goes rushing out of the back of the engine. The air blows toward the back of the plane. The engine moves in the opposite direction of the air—the engine moves forward. The engine is on the wing, so the wing moves forward. The wing is on the plane, so the plane moves forward. **(B)** ✻ 2 ERRORS ✻

Here's the rule about jet engines: **The air blows toward the back. The plane moves the opposite way.** **(C)**

Touch the jet engine in the picture. **(D)**

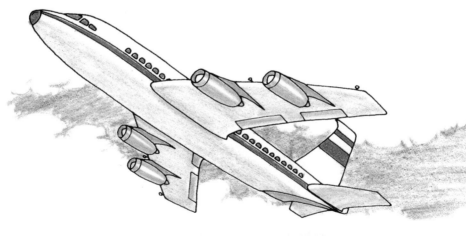

Show how the air rushes out of the jet engine. **(E)**

Show which way the plane will move. **(F)**

When jet engines work, they make a great, loud sound. The plane goes down the runway, faster and faster. The people inside try to act as if they are not frightened, but their hearts start pounding faster.Ⓖ The people begin to wonder how a plane that is almost as big as a school can take off and fly like a bird. Racing cars go two hundred miles per hour. The jet plane goes faster than most racing cars before its nose lifts up and it takes off.Ⓗ

Then the passengers look out the windows and have trouble believing what they see. They see their city, but it looks like a toy city—with tiny cars and buildings that look so small you could pick them up.Ⓘ The plane circles around, and the passengers look at the buildings in downtown New York. "Wow," they say to themselves.Ⓙ

Then the plane goes up and up until it is six miles above the ground. Think of it. Six miles high.Ⓚ

Now, a flight attendant talks to the passengers. "You may remove your seat belts and you may move around the plane now, but you may not smoke while you're standing or walking."Ⓛ The passengers start to talk to each other now. They feel safe. The plane doesn't seem to be moving at all. Walking around inside the plane is just like walking around inside a building. But the passengers inside the plane are moving along at the speed of 5 hundred miles per hour.Ⓜ

Herman was moving at 5 hundred miles per hour. But he wasn't thinking much about it. He didn't feel like a super fly. In fact, he wasn't the only fly in that jumbo jet. Like most jumbo jets that fly in the summer, it had flies in it. There were six flies and one beetle.Ⓝ 🌼 9 ERRORS 🌼

LESSON 50

A

1	2	3
degrees	Denver	Chicago
ocean	captain	gentle
facing	huge	heaven
panel	metal	galley

4

Michigan
shrimp
happened
perfect
dodge

5

Vocabulary words

1. couple of times
2. brew

B

DEGREES

When an object gets hotter, what happens to the temperature of the object?Ⓐ

We measure temperature in degrees.Ⓑ
Here's the rule: **When the temperature goes up, the number of degrees goes up.**Ⓒ

Look at the picture. It tells how many degrees each object is.Ⓓ

A **40 degrees**   B **10 degrees**   C **70 degrees**

The hottest object is the object with the biggest number of degrees.Ⓔ

Which object is the hottest?Ⓕ

Which object is next-hottest?Ⓖ

Which object is the coldest?Ⓗ

On a hot summer day, the air may reach 38 degrees. On a cold winter day when cars won't start, the air may get down to 30 degrees below zero.

The temperature inside your school is about 20 degrees.

C

1	2	3
bounced	engine	taxi
airport	important	flew
chew	runway	whole
passenger	decision	realized
worry	above	crawled
remind	refrigerator	sunlight
peaceful	actually	farther
complained	crew	worried
San Francisco	repeated	brightly
couple	prove	meant
regular	between	purse
city	temperature	believe
together	neither	downtown
speedometer	thrown	moving
expression	cabbage	busy

LESSON 51

A

1	2	3
fasten	head	galley
copilot	cleared	metal
	reaching	Denver
	cleaned	heaven
	ready	panel

4	5	6
brewing	captain	huge
Michigan	happened	direction
shrimp	gentle	facing
Chicago	ocean	blown
perfect		dodge

7

Vocabulary words

1. meal service
2. couple of times
3. brew

B

Herman Lands in San Francisco Ⓐ

Sometimes flies get on jumbo jets. And
sometimes these flies will go all the way across
the United States. That's what happened to
Herman. He went from a city on the east coast to
a city on the west coast. Ⓑ And he wasn't the
only fly on that trip. Ⓒ

When the plane was over Chicago, the
captain talked over the loud-speaker to the
passengers. "Look below and you can see the
city of Chicago. That lake you see next to
Chicago is Lake Michigan." Ⓓ

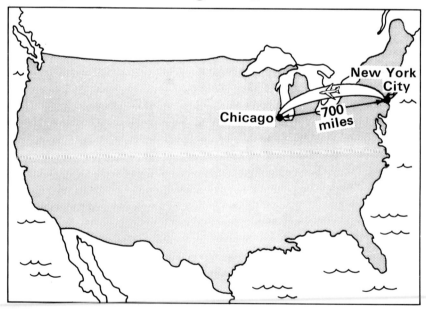

Herman wasn't looking at any lakes. He was trying to find something to eat. He could smell some really good stuff. ❋ 2 ERRORS ❋

The crew was brewing coffee and cooking dinner for the passengers. It didn't take Herman very long to find the place where the food was. On a plane, that place is not called a kitchen. It is called a galley.Ⓔ The galley was warm, and it smelled great to Herman.

"We're going to begin our meal service now," a crew member said. "So please return to your seats." Ⓕ

Herman had already started his meal service. Ⓖ He started with a salad that had some shrimp on it. Ⓗ "Good," he thought to himself. Then he went to a piece of cheese. "Good, good," he thought to himself. Ⓘ Did that fly ever eat!

When the meal service was over, it was time for a nap. Herman found the perfect place. It was a metal panel next to the oven. Ⓙ It was very warm—just right.

Herman napped for the rest of the trip. The crew members put away the food trays. They cleaned up the galley, and Herman had to get out of their way a couple of times. But he flew back to his nice warm metal panel and had a good rest. The trip from New York City to San Francisco took six hours. Ⓚ After the plane passed over Chicago, it went west over Denver, and then over Salt Lake City. And then it landed in San Francisco. Touch the cities the plane passed over: Chicago, Denver, Salt Lake City. Ⓛ

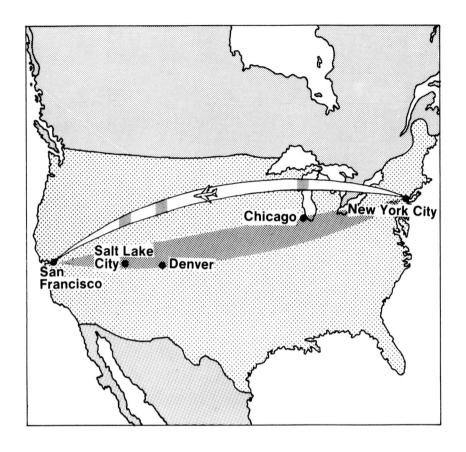

When the plane landed in San Francisco, the passengers got off and said thank you to the crew members. Then the crew members got off and said, "Am I glad to be home." Ⓜ Then three flies got off. Ⓝ And then four men and three women came on the plane and cleaned up. They also filled the air with a spray that kills flies. Ⓞ ✻ 8 ERRORS ✻

LESSON 52

1	2	3
enemy	facing	fasten
Pacific	ocean	copilot
caught	gentle	continue
Japan	direction	fastened
continue	blown	

4	5	6
enemy	corners	**Vocabulary words**
caught	closet	**1.** gate
Pacific	attention	**2.** flight
Japan	closets	**3.** thaw
		4. breeze

B

Finding the Direction of a Wind

To find the direction of a wind, you face the wind so the wind blows in your face. Ⓐ

The direction you're facing tells about the wind. If you face east, the wind is an east wind. If you face north, the wind is a north wind. Ⓑ

Look at picture A. The arrows show the wind. The cow is facing into the wind. Which direction is the cow facing? Ⓒ So what's the name of the wind? Ⓓ

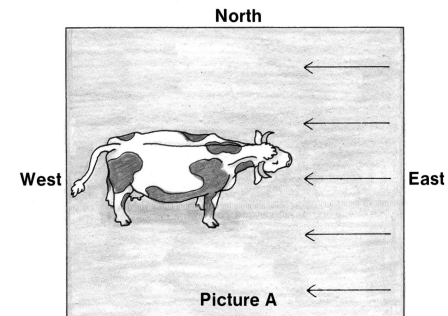

Picture A

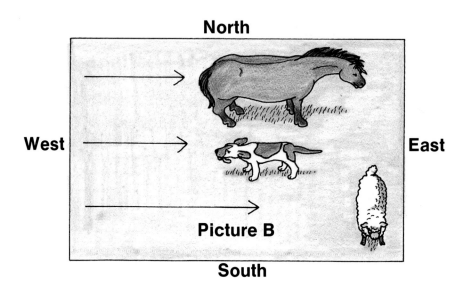

North

West

East

Picture B

South

Look at picture B. The arrows show the wind. Which animal is facing into the wind?Ⓔ Which direction is that animal facing?Ⓕ So what's the name of the wind?Ⓖ

C

Fly Spray Fills the AirⒶ

Herman and five other flies were on the Jumbo Jet when it landed in San Francisco. Some of them got off the plane in San Francisco.Ⓑ Shortly after the plane pulled up to the gate, some men and women came into the plane and cleaned it. They filled the air with fly spray.Ⓒ When the air cleared and the workers left the plane, there were two dead flies.**(D)** One fly felt quite well. This fly had been sitting on a warm metal panel in the galley.**(E)** That panel was close to an outside door. Two workers had opened that door and then started to load up the dinners for the next flight.**(F)** ❁ 2 ERRORS ❁

The workers stacked the dinners next to Herman. The dinners didn't smell very good because they were frozen, and flies do not like things that are too cold. Fresh air blew in through the open door. This air kept the fly spray from reaching Herman. Herman didn't know that the air saved his life. While it was blowing on him, he kept thinking, "This air is too cold. I should fly to a warmer place."**(G)** Every time he got ready to take off, the air stopped blowing so hard and he could feel the nice warm panel. So he made a decision to stay on the metal panel.**(H)**

If the air in San Francisco had been warmer, Herman might never have become the fly who flew farther than any other fly.**(I)** You know what Herman would have done if he'd felt a nice warm breeze and if he'd felt sunlight outside.**(J)** But San Francisco weather is usually pretty cool. Here is why: San Francisco is next to the ocean. The air over the ocean is cool. The air blows from the ocean to San Francisco.Ⓚ So, San Francisco is cool.

Touch the X on the map.Ⓛ That is where the wind starts.

Touch San Francisco.Ⓜ

If you were in San Francisco, which direction would you face if you wanted the wind to blow in your face?Ⓝ

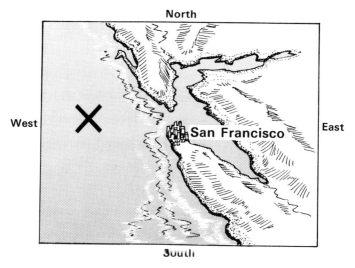

The jet that Herman was on was going back to New York City. That jet would go faster on the trip to New York City. Here's why. The jet was going to fly in the same direction the wind was blowing.Ⓞ   ❋ 7 ERRORS ❋

LESSON 53

A

1	**2**	**3**
distance	fastened	closets
poisonous	blown	attention
excitement	caught	Pacific
label	Japan	corners
Ohio		

4	**5**	**6**
catch	place	**Vocabulary words**
mark	Alaska	1. loud-speaker
catching	enemy	2. rough air
marked	placed	3. dodge
catches	continue	4. copilot
		5. huge
		6. thaw

Airplanes and Wind

Look at the pictures below.

All the planes in the picture can go
5 hundred miles per hour if there is no wind.
But there is a wind in each picture.Ⓐ

 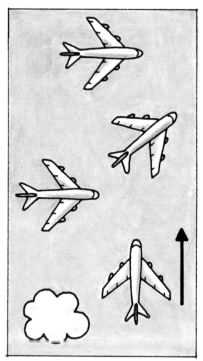

Picture 1   **Picture 2**

Here's the rule: **The planes go the fastest
when they go in the same direction the wind
is blowing.** Ⓑ

C

A Rough Trip Ⓐ

Although Herman reached San Francisco in the middle of June, the air was cool because it was coming from a cool place. Ⓑ When Herman's jet landed, the temperature was only 24 degrees. An hour later, the temperature was 16 degrees, and the jet was ready to fly back to New York City. Ⓒ

A strong wind was blowing from the west. That wind was pushing big storm clouds over the United States. The captain of the jet plane knew about these clouds. He also knew that the jet would not be able to dodge them. The passengers were in for some rough air.

❈ 2 ERRORS ❈

The captain said to his copilot, who sat next to him, "We're going to have some frightened passengers before this trip is over." Ⓓ

The captain was right. Ⓔ The jet took off and circled over the ocean. Then it turned and headed toward New York City. Ⓕ The jet began to climb higher and higher. Then it reached the huge clouds that had been blown in by the strong west wind. "Ladies and gentlemen," the captain said over the loud-speaker. "Please stay in your seat and keep your seat belt fastened. We are going to run into some rough . . . " **G** The plane suddenly bounced. Then it dropped. "Oh," some of the people said. **H** They began to hang onto their seats. The plane bounced again

and again. It seemed as if the plane was going over a very, very rough road. Some of the passengers looked at the wings. The wings were bouncing up and down. A lot of the passengers were thinking the same thing.ⓘ They thought, "We're going to crash," but they didn't say that. They tried to look brave. "This air is rough," they said with a smile.ⓙ But they were not smiling inside.Ⓚ

The crew on the plane didn't mind the rough air very much. They knew that they would be out of the rough air as soon as they got above the clouds. They weren't the only ones who were not afraid.Ⓛ Herman had found a candy wrapper. And it was good, good, GOOD. The plane was much warmer now. And the food in the ovens was starting to thaw out.Ⓜ So the food was smelling good, good, GOOD. And while the passengers were thinking, "I'm going to be sick," Herman was thinking, "This place is good, good, GOOD."

The trip going to San Francisco had taken six hours.Ⓝ The trip back to New York took only five hours.

Can you figure out why?Ⓞ ❋ 8 ERRORS ❋

LESSON 54

A

1	2	3	4
Texas	Pacific	label	distance
camera	enemy	attention	excitement
compare	closets	corner	sweat
California	caught	poisonous	exit
dead	Japan	labeled	Ohio

5	6	7
shove	catching	**Vocabulary words**
visit	marked	**1.** catch your attention
shoved	Alaska	**2.** continue
visiting	catches	
fifty	placed	

B

More about the Globe

In today's story you will read about a trip from New York City to San Francisco and then to Japan.Ⓐ The map on the next page shows that trip.

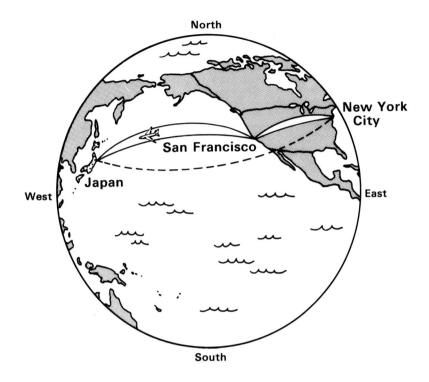

Touch New York City and go to San Francisco. **B** In which direction do you go? **C**

Now go from San Francisco to Japan. **D** In which direction do you go? **E**

Which is farther, the trip from New York City to San Francisco or the trip from San Francisco to Japan? **F**

Your teacher will show you a globe of the world. Find New York City on that globe. Then go west from New York City to San Francisco. Then go west from San Francisco to Japan. **G**

C

HERman Heaðs for Japan Ⓐ

The jumbo jet landed at Kennedy Airport five hours after it took off from San Francisco. Ⓑ The passengers got off the plane, and the crew got off the plane. Workers came and sprayed the inside of the plane with insect spray. Ⓒ After the air cleared, there were six dead flies and one dead ant in the plane. Ⓓ But there was still one living fly. That fly had crawled inside one of the ovens. Ⓔ The oven had cooled some, but it was nice and warm.

By that evening the oven was cool, and Herman crawled out. Passengers were coming into the plane. 🌸 2 ERRORS 🌸

Some of the passengers were going to San Francisco. But some of them were going a lot farther. They were on their way to Japan. Ⓕ The jumbo jet was going to fly to San Francisco, and then it was going to continue to Japan. Ⓖ After leaving San Francisco, the jet was going to cross a great ocean, called the Pacific Ocean. Ⓗ The trip from New York City to San Francisco is 25 hundred miles. After leaving San Francisco, a plane must fly west for another 45 hundred miles to get to Japan. Ⓘ

Look at the map. It shows the world. Touch New York City on the map, and follow the jet's trip to San Francisco and then on to Japan. Ⓙ In which direction did the plane go? Ⓚ

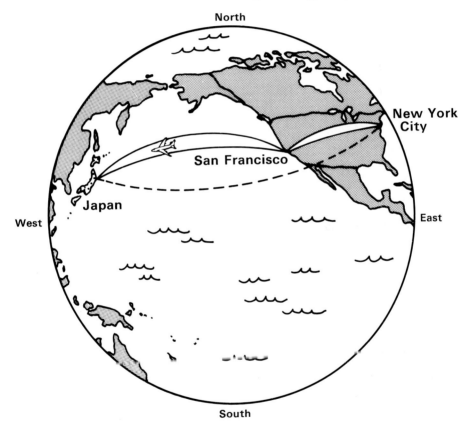

*After the plane left San Francisco, the passengers napped and talked and ate. While they did that, Herman met an enemy. Ⓛ

Herman was buzzing around near one of the coat closets in the jumbo jet. It was dark inside the coat closets, but some smells caught Herman's attention, so Herman buzzed inside one of the closets.Ⓜ He buzzed up into one of the corners. And then he kept trying to fly, but his legs were stuck to something.Ⓝ He buzzed his wings harder and harder. But he couldn't pull himself free. Once more, he buzzed. Time to rest.Ⓞ

Herman, like* other flies, had big strange eyes that could see in all directions at the same time. Suddenly, Herman's eyes saw something moving toward him very fast. It was a large hairy thing with eight legs and a mean-looking mouth.Ⓟ Herman was stuck in a spider web, and the spider was ready to eat dinner.Ⓠ

✿ 8 ERRORS ✿

LESSON 55

A

1	2	3
dries	labeled	marked
fries	Ohio	catches
cries	dead	robins
dies	flies	Alaska
tries	butterflies	catching

4	5	6
California	sweat	passenger
placed	visiting	copilot
compare	shoved	temperature
camera	Texas	Michigan
exit	fifty	

7	8	9
continue	poisonous	attention
Pacific	realized	Chicago
excitement	lifetime	enemy
actually	believing	together

B

THE EYE OF A FLY

If you look at a drop of water, you will see little pictures of things in the drop.

Look at this drop. You can see a window and a light in the drop.Ⓐ

Your eye works like a drop. It is round and it catches pictures the same way the water drop catches pictures.

Look at the picture of the eye. You can see the picture the eye is catching.Ⓑ

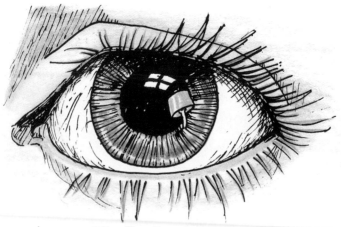

A fly's eye is different from a human eye. Look at the fly in the picture. Below the fly is a large picture of the fly's eye. ⓒ

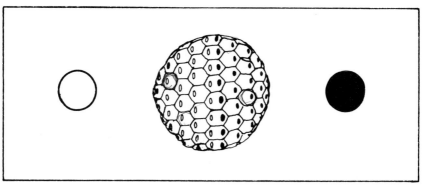

The eye of a fly is made up of many, many drops. Each drop catches a picture.

The fly is catching pictures of a white dot and a black dot.

Some drops on the eye catch a picture of only the black dot.

Some drops catch a picture of only the white dot.

Some drops catch a picture of both dots. ⓓ

C

The Size of Some States

The United States is a country.Ⓐ It is called the United States because it is made up of many states. There are fifty states in the United States.Ⓑ The map shows the states that are in the United States. Four states are labeled.Ⓒ

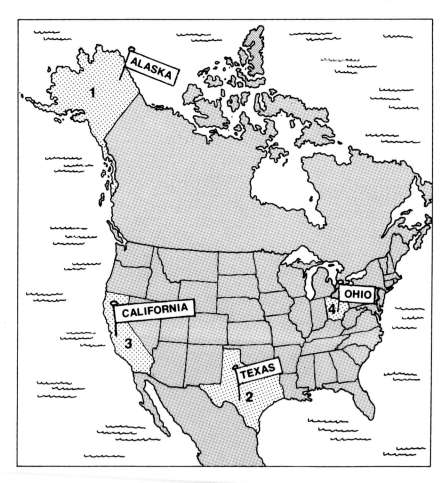

The state that is marked **1** is Alaska. It is the biggest state in the United States.Ⓓ

State 2 is Texas. It is the second biggest state.Ⓔ

State 3 is the third biggest state. What is the name of that state?Ⓕ

State 4 is one of the smaller states. Its name is Ohio.Ⓖ   ❋ 2 ERRORS ❋

The United States is much bigger than the country of Japan.Ⓗ The whole country of Japan is smaller than the state of Alaska.Ⓘ Here's a picture of what the whole country of Japan would look like if it were placed next to Alaska.Ⓙ   ❋ 4 ERRORS ❋

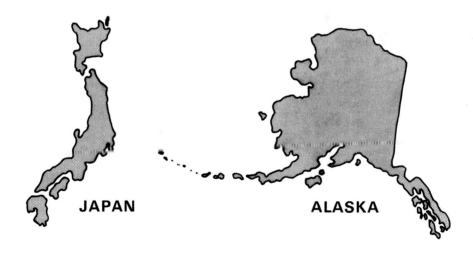

JAPAN   **ALASKA**

LESSON 56

A

1	2	3
aisle	excitement	China
Italy	distance	camera
million	poisonous	visiting
warm-blooded	compared	cameras
cold-blooded		robins

4	5	6
dead	circle	**Vocabulary words**
shoved	travel	**1.** mummy
sweat	Turkey	**2.** compare
exit	circled	
butterflies	traveled	

B

FACTS ABOUT SPIDERS

In the last Herman story, Herman met an enemy. What kind of animal was that enemy? Ⓐ

Here are facts about spiders:

- Spiders are not insects. Ⓑ
- Spiders have eight legs, not six legs. Ⓒ
- Many spiders make webs to catch insects. Ⓓ
- Some spiders are bigger than your fist. Ⓔ
- Most spiders are not poisonous to people. Ⓕ

Herman Tries to Escape Ⓐ

Herman was tired from trying to escape from the spider web, but when his eyes saw a big hairy spider moving toward him, Herman found a lot of strength. Ⓑ He buzzed harder than he had ever buzzed before. He tugged and pulled against the web. The web was sticky and it didn't let go of Herman's legs. But Herman kept trying.

Now the spider was grabbing Herman. The spider was much bigger than Herman—three times bigger. Ⓒ The spider could walk on the web without getting stuck. But Herman was

really stuck. And the spider was trying to bite Herman and trying to wrap him up in a web.(D)

2 ERRORS

Most spiders kill insects by biting them. Then they wrap the insects in a web. The insect looks like a mummy.(E) Later, the spider comes back and eats the best parts of the dead insect. The spider leaves the rest of the insect hanging in the web.(F)

The passengers in the jumbo jet were talking to each other or leaning back in their seats thinking about what they would do when they reached Japan.(G) Once in a while, passengers would look below at the ocean.(H) They would think that the ocean would never end.(I) The passengers would think, "Ocean, ocean, ocean. All you can see is ocean. No land, no buildings, just ocean." While the passengers sat and talked and thought, Herman was fighting for his life.(J)

Herman was lucky. The spider tried to turn Herman around and wrap him up. But when the spider turned Herman, the spider freed Herman's legs from the web.(K) Herman gave a great buzz with his wings. He gave the hardest buzz he could make. Suddenly, he was in the air, with some sticky stuff still on his legs. Ⓛ

Get out of that dark, Herman thought. Ⓜ He flew from the closet to the bright parts of the jet. A moment later, Herman landed on a warm red and rubbed his front legs together. Ⓝ As Herman sat on the seat back, he did not remember what had just happened. For Herman, things were warm and red. And he was tired. Time to nap. Ⓞ

For the passengers it was time for excitement. Look off in the distance. The green strips of land and a great mountain. "Look," they said as they crowded near the windows, "Japan." Ⓟ

Now the passengers began to get ready for the plane's landing. ⓠ Some people fixed their hair. Others put away their pens and papers. Every few moments, they looked out the windows again. "It's beautiful," they said. It was. As the passengers felt this excitement, Herman slept. ⓡ ✹ 9 ERRORS ✹

LESSON 57

A

1	**2**	**3**
fuel	service	robins
frost	cameras	compared
Hohoboho	visiting	shoved
worst	sweat	million
telephone	serviced	Italy

4	**5**	**6**
butterflies	traveled	**Vocabulary words**
aisle	warm-blooded	1. exit door
circled	China	2. shove
Turkey	cold-blooded	3. compare
garbage		

B The Jumbo Jet Lands in Japan ⓐ

Japan is a small country compared to the United States. ⓑ But many people live in Japan. Japan is smaller than the state of Alaska. But there are more people in Japan than there are in these three states put together: Texas, Alaska, and Ohio.

The passengers on the plane lined up and pushed and shoved and crowded toward the exit door. ⓒ Many people were going home. Others were visiting Japan. Some of them planned to buy cameras.

Through this excitement, Herman slept. He slept until the plane became cool. ⓓ

You know that flies don't like cool weather. You can understand why flies don't like the cool weather if you understand how flies are different from humans or dogs. ⓔ ❋ 2 ERRORS ❋

Flies are insects. All insects are cold-blooded. So flies are cold-blooded. ⓕ

Cold-blooded animals are different from warm-blooded animals. ⓖ Here are some animals that are warm-blooded: robins, dogs, rabbits, cows, humans, horses, and deer. ⓗ

Here are some animals that are cold-blooded: ants, fleas, water striders, spiders, and butterflies. Ⓘ

If an animal is warm-blooded, the temperature inside that animal's body always stays the same. Ⓙ If the outside temperature goes up, the inside temperature does not change. Ⓚ If the outside temperature goes down, the inside temperature does not change. Ⓛ

If an animal is cold-blooded, the inside temperature of that animal changes when the outside temperature changes. Ⓜ If the outside temperature goes up, what happens to the inside temperature? Ⓝ

If the outside temperature goes down, what happens to the inside temperature? Ⓞ

Your body temperature is always around 98.6 degrees. Ⓟ When the air outside is 15 degrees below zero, your fingers may get cold. Your feet may feel very cold. But the inside of your body is 98.6 degrees. Ⓠ When the temperature outside is 109 degrees, you may feel very warm and sticky. You may sweat. Ⓡ But the inside of your body is still 98.6 degrees.

Flies are different. Their inside temperature

changes as the temperature outside their body changes. ⓢ When the air is 109̶4̶8̶ degrees outside, the inside of the fly is 109̶4̶8̶ degrees. When the air is 60̶1̶6̶ degrees outside, you know the temperature inside the fly. ⓣ

Because flies work this way, they have a problem: Their body slows down when it gets cold. ⓤ Try catching a fly on a warm day. It is hard to do because the fly is fast. The fly is fast because everything inside the fly's body is working fast. ⓥ

Try catching a fly outside when the weather is very cool. ⓦ The fly is slow and easy to catch. The fly is slow because everything inside the fly's body is working very slowly. Remember: A fly's body slows down when it gets cold. ⓧ

Herman didn't know this rule. He did know that he didn't like cool places and he didn't like dark places unless they were warm. He wanted to get out of the jet because it was getting too cool for him. The air temperature was down to 16 degrees. ⓨ He was slowing down. And his eyes could see that something was coming toward him. ⓩ ❀ 10 ERRORS ❀

LESSON 58

1	2	3
Italy	Hohoboho	circled
aisle	fuel	garbage
million	China	serviced
telephone	traveled	strange
worst	Turkey	strangest

4	5
hooray	**Vocabulary words**
happy	frost
happiest	
noise	
noisier	

B

The Air around the Earth

Here's a rule about the temperature of the air around the earth: **When you go higher, the temperature gets lower.** Ⓐ

Let's say that the temperature on the ground is 68 degrees. You go up 1 mile.

The temperature is now less than 68 degrees. It may be only 60 degrees.

You go up another mile. Ⓑ The temperature is less than 60 degrees. It's 32 degrees. Ⓒ

Use the rule about temperature to answer these questions:

Tom is 1 mile high.

Jerry is 3 miles high.

Who is colder? Ⓓ

Why? Ⓔ

C

Herman Flies to Italy Ⓐ

Herman was on a seat back of a jumbo jet. The inside of the plane had become very cold. Ⓑ

Herman watched a big dark move toward him. Ⓒ Herman tried to get out of the way, but his legs would hardly move. Very slowly, he crawled into a crack on the seat back. The big dark moved past him. Then another big dark moved past. The big darks were really crew members, getting ready for the next flight. They were walking down an aisle of the plane. Ⓓ

Herman was on a seat right next to the
aisle. ❋ 2 ERRORS ❋

The crew members walked right past
Herman. Ⓔ One crew member was wearing a
coat that brushed against the spot where
Herman had been. But Herman was in the crack
of the seat, feeling very slow, very slow.

Then Herman began to feel faster. Ⓕ He
could move his front feet faster. He peeked out of

the crack and noticed that the plane was brighter now. He thought about flying, but it was too cold for that. So he crawled out on the seat and waited and waited. (G)

By the time the passengers got on the plane, Herman was able to fly fairly fast. The plane was now 64 degrees. Some of the passengers said, "Oh, my, it's cold in this plane." When the plane moved down the runway, the inside of the plane was 69 degrees, and Herman was flying very fast. (H) He was feeling quite good now and was looking for good things to smell and eat.

The plane took off and went up six miles. The inside of the plane was still 69 degrees. (I) But the outside air was now 57 degrees below zero. (J) The captain talked over the loud-speaker and told the passengers about the temperature outside the plane. "Wow," some of the passengers said. Herman said, "Bzz," as he headed toward the galley. (K)

The captain told the passengers, "Look at your map and you can follow our flight today. We left Japan and we're flying straight to Italy. (L) We will fly over China and Turkey on our way to Italy. (M) The flight to Italy is six

thousand miles and should take 16 hours."
Touch Japan on the map and follow the
plane's flight. **O**

The country of Italy is very small compared to the United States.Ⓟ Italy is smaller than the state of Alaska.Ⓠ Italy is small, but a lot of people live in Italy—60 million people live there.Ⓡ

Italy is shaped something like a boot.Ⓢ

The jumbo jet circled several times and then landed. The passengers cheered and waved as they got off the plane. Nobody cheered for Herman. But Herman had just traveled farther than any other insect that ever lived.Ⓣ

 9 ERRORS

LESSON 59

1	2	3
relative	fuel	whoop
confusion	serviced	happiest
	garbage	long
	strangest	belong
	noisier	whooping
	hooray	

4
Vocabulary words
frost

B

A Man and His Pets

A man had five fleas. When those fleas lined up end to end, they were _____ long.

The man had a pencil. It was a short pencil. So it weighed _____.

The man had three dogs. Two of them were the same size. They were a poodle and a pointer. They were _____ long. The third dog the man had looked something like a pointer, but it was shorter. It was brown and white and black. That dog could have been a

_____.

When the man went places without his car, he sometimes moved 20 miles per hour. Was he running or walking?

One of his dogs could run faster than he could. This dog could run 35 miles per hour. What kind of dog was it?

Sometimes the man would go in something that moved 5 hundred miles per hour. What did he go in?

These jets are so fast that they can fly from New York City to San Francisco in _____ hours. The flight from New York City to San Francisco is _____ miles.

C

Herman's Last Trip Ⓐ

Herman ate and slept and felt warm and napped and smelled good things. For Herman, there was light and there was dark. There were things that smelled good and things that smelled bad.Ⓑ There were warm things and cold things. He didn't know that he had traveled farther than any other insect. And he didn't know that the plane was on its way back to New York City.Ⓒ

The plane had landed in Italy. Passengers got off and passengers got on. The crew got off and a new crew got on. People serviced the plane. They checked the tires and filled the plane with jet fuel. ❋ 2 ERRORS ❋

Do you know where the gas tanks are on a big jet? They are in the wings.Ⓓ All the parts of the plane were checked.Ⓔ Then the plane took off. It was on its way back to an airport that Herman had seen before.Ⓕ

Look at the map. It shows the last part of the jet's trip.Ⓖ

Herman had gone west from New York City and west from San Francisco and west from

Japan. Now Herman went west from Italy. And
Herman was on his way back to New York City.
By going west, Herman had gone all the way
around the world. **H**

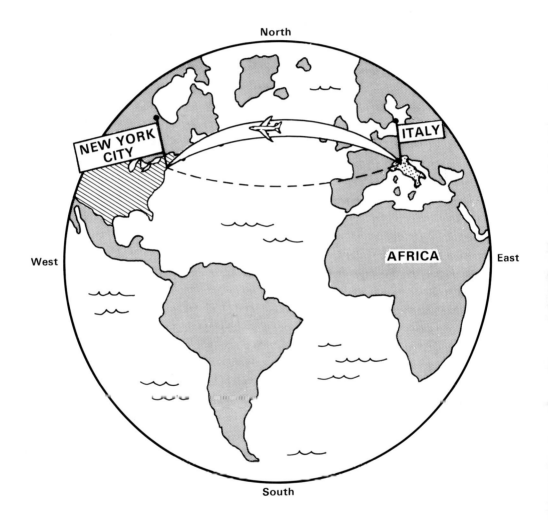

When the plane landed in New York City, Herman caught a good smell and followed it. He left the plane. For the next couple of hours he buzzed around inside the airport. Then he went outside. It was hot and the air was filled with good smells. He landed on top of an airport bus. And that bus stopped a few blocks from the place where Herman was born. Herman didn't know that he had come back to his home. He just knew that the sun felt very good and that it was time to eat. So he ate. For the rest of the summer, he buzzed around with other flies, doing the things that flies do.ⓘ He bothered people, and he joined crowds of flies in garbage cans and other smelly places. He had a good time.

Then the days became colder and colder, and it was harder for Herman to move around.Ⓙ Summer was over.Ⓚ It was fall now. Every now and then, a warm day would make Herman feel frisky again, but most of the time, he moved very slowly.Ⓛ

One night early in November, the temperature dropped below freezing.Ⓜ The low temperature killed Herman and millions of other flies. The next morning people woke up and looked outside. They saw frost sparkling on the sidewalks and on the cars. "Look at the frost," they said. "It's beautiful." But for Herman there would be no more beautiful things—no smells and bright lights. There would be no fear of spiders. The insect that had traveled farther than any other insect was dead.

But Herman had a lot of children. In fact, the next spring, when the days got warm, Herman's 8 thousand children were born. They were maggots, and they looked just like Herman had looked when he was a maggot. And many of these maggots grew up to be flies, just like Herman. The next time you look at a fly, take a good look. Maybe that fly is one of Herman's children. (N) ❋ 11 ERRORS ❋

LESSON 60

1	2	3	4
worst	strangest	relative	hooray
wonder	telephone	confusion	belong
wander	Hohoboho	happiest	whooping
word	noisier	relatives	six
world			sixth
want			

5	6
fifteen	bound
nine	seven
ninth	bounding
fifteenth	seventh

B

The World of Hohoboho Ⓐ

This is a story about a sad word that lived in a make-believe world called Hohoboho. Ⓑ The words in Hohoboho were not like the words in our world. And the people in Hohoboho were not like the people in our world. These people talked, but they didn't do anything else. Ⓒ The people didn't read. They didn't play baseball.

They didn't eat. They didn't even sing. All they did was talk. Ⓓ

Here's the strangest part about Hohoboho. Every time a person said a word, that word felt happy. Ⓔ

Words that were said a lot were very, very happy. ❋ 2 ERRORS ❋

Words that were said quite a bit were happy part of the time. Ⓕ

Words that were said only once in a while were sort of sad.

The rest of the words were very sad.

How often were these words said? Ⓖ

The word in our story was hardly ever said. So you know how that word felt. Ⓗ

All words in Hohoboho stayed in a strange place called the word bank. Ⓘ There were over one hundred rows in the word bank.

The best seats in the word bank were in front. The very happy words sat in these seats. The words that were hardly ever said sat in the back of the word bank. These were the worst seats. Ⓙ The words in the front were always yelling and cheering. Ⓚ Every time somebody used one of them, the word would jump up and yell, "I'm the best," or "Hooray for me." Here are some of the words that sat in the best seats of the word bank: **me, am, what, who, is, we, I, not.** You can think of other words that might be in the first rows of the word bank by thinking of the words that you say all the time. You say the word **me** and the word **you.** You say the word **here** and the word **there.** You say the word **have** and the word **had.** Name some other words that you say all the time. Ⓛ

Words that were sort of happy sat in the middle rows of the word bank. Ⓜ These words were said quite a bit but not as often as words like **you** and **how.** Here are some words that sat in the middle: **should, other, telephone. Ⓝ** These words didn't yell and shout all day long. But they were a lot noisier than the words in the back. Ⓞ Every now and then one of the words in the middle of the word bank would jump up and say, "That's me." Ⓟ

With all the yelling and shouting, the word bank was very loud.

Which part of the bank was the loudest? Ⓠ

Which part was sort of loud? Ⓡ

Which part was pretty quiet? Ⓢ

The back of the bank was so quiet that a whole day might pass without one sound from the back of the bank. Ⓣ

The words that sat near the back of the word bank were words that you wouldn't say very often. Here are some words that sat near the back: **confusion, fifteenth, mummy.** Name some other words that sat near the back of the word bank. Ⓤ

You'll never guess which words sat in the very last rows of the word bank. ❋ 11 ERRORS ❋

LESSON 61

A

1	2	3	4
special	ninth	whooping	lifeboat
bulkhead	seventh	belong	prow
neighbor	fifteenth	bounding	Friday
amazing	sixth	Thursday	lifeboats

5

silent

ever

forever

happy

happier

6

Vocabulary words

1. thrown into confusion
2. relatives
3. whoop

B

Liz Takes a Trip

Liz liked cool weather. It was the middle of summer, and she wanted to go to a city that was cool in the summer. So she went to the city of _____.

Liz knew that the temperature of an object tells how _____ that object is. When she left New York City, the air on the ground was 30 degrees. But when the plane went higher and higher, the air outside the plane got _____.

When the plane was 6 miles high, the air outside the plane was below zero. It was _____.

When the plane went from New York City to San Francisco, it was going in which direction?

The plane was facing the wind, so the name of the wind was a _____.

Did the plane go faster or slower than a plane going in the opposite direction?

The air that rushed from the jet engines was going to the east, so the jet engines moved toward the _____. The jet engines were attached to parts of the plane. Those parts were the _____.

As Liz flew along, she wanted to get a good look at things on the ground below. So she looked through something that makes things look very big. She looked through _____. She saw the city of

Chicago. That city was between Denver and

_____ .

In San Francisco, Liz saw a lot of animals at a zoo. She knew how tall each animal was.

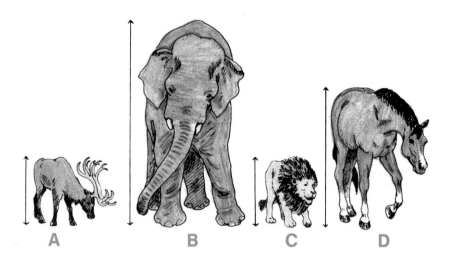

A   B   C   D

C

The Words That Sat in the Back Rows Ⓐ

The words that sat in the back of the word bank didn't have much fun. Ⓑ They tried not to listen to the other words yelling and cheering, but they couldn't help it. They wanted to be said more often. Every now and then one of the words in front would turn around and say something like, "Look at those words in the back of the bank. They aren't any good at all."

The word in our story sat in the very last row of the word bank. Ⓒ The word was **run.**

 2 ERRORS

If we had a word bank in our world, the word **run** would not sit in the back row. Ⓓ But you must remember that the people in Hohoboho did not do anything. So they didn't talk much about doing things. They didn't talk about running or jumping or walking. You know other things they didn't talk about very much. Ⓔ

So the word **run** sat in the last row. The word **run** sat behind words like **speedometer** and **temperature.** The word **run** sat behind.

words like **maggots, enough, binoculars,** and **direction. Run** sat next to its relatives. One relative was the word **runner.** Another relative was the word **ran.** You know some of the other relatives of **run. Ⓕ**

Next to the **run** family sat the **walk** family. You know some of the relatives of **walk** that were in that family.**Ⓖ** And next to that family was the **jump** family, and then the **ride** family, and the **eat** family.**Ⓗ**

Every once in a while, one of the words from the back row would try to sit closer to the front of the word bank.**Ⓘ** Look at the picture. Two words are sitting in the wrong seats.**Ⓙ**

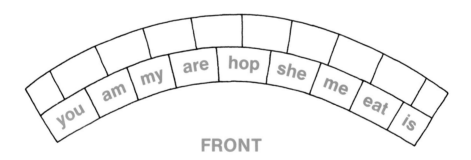

FRONT

This trick didn't work because the other words always caught the sad words. "Hey, you can't move up here," they would say. "Go back to the last row and sit where you belong." So the sad words would sit and wait and hope.Ⓚ Once in a while, somebody would say their names and they would feel good, very good. They tried to remember how good they felt. Sometimes, they would talk about it. The word **runner** liked to say, "I remember one day when my name was said four times. Four times in one day."Ⓛ

The other sad words got tired of hearing this story. They would say, "Oh, be quiet. You just got lucky. You usually don't have your name said once a month."

"Yeah," one of the other sad words would say. "You don't get said any more often than the rest of us."

"It will happen again," **runner** would reply. "You'll see. One of these days, they're going to start saying my name all the time. I'll bet I get to move up five rows. You'll see."

"Oh, be quiet."Ⓜ

Then the sad words would sit back and feel sad. Long day after long day, they would sit and try not to listen to those words in the front of the bank whooping and howling.Ⓝ ❋ 10 ERRORS ❋

LESSON 62

A

1	2	3	4
announce	bulkhead	sixth	neighbor
notice	forever	prow	seventh
occasionally	lifeboats	ninth	Thursday
effort	outline	Friday	neighbors

5	6	7	8
special	thirsty	squeeze	current
fifteenth	thirstier	tumble	begin
happier	easy	stumble	beginner
silent	easier	squeezed	currents
		stumbled	beginning

9

Vocabulary words

1. bounding
2. announcement
3. great
4. amazing
5. thrown into confusion

B Facts about an Ocean Liner

The story that you will read in a few days tells about an ocean liner. Ⓐ Here are facts about an ocean liner:

- An ocean liner is a very large ship. Ⓑ
- An ocean liner is made to carry passengers. Ⓒ
- Special ship names are used to talk about parts of an ocean liner.

The front of the ship is called the **prow.** Ⓓ The prow in the picture is marked with a **P.** Touch the prow. Ⓔ The back of the ship is called the **stern.** Ⓕ The stern is marked with an **S.** Touch the stern. Ⓖ The floors are called **decks.** Ⓗ One deck is marked with a **D.** Touch that deck. Ⓘ The walls are called **bulkheads.** Ⓙ One wall is marked with a **B.** Touch that bulkhead. Ⓚ

Notice that the ocean liner in the picture is 200 meters long. Ⓛ

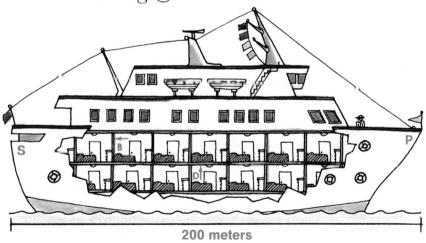

200 meters

C The Big Change in Hohoboho Ⓐ

Every Friday, words in the word bank were moved. Sometimes the people in Hohoboho started to say a word more often. On Friday, that word would be moved closer to the front of the word bank. Ⓑ

The opposite also happened. Ⓒ If a word was not said as often as it had been said, it was moved toward the back of the word bank. Ⓓ A lot of words would be moved around every Friday, but they were usually moved only one or two rows. The word **eraser** was usually in the sixth row, but every now and then it would move up as far as the fourth row or as far back as the ninth row. ❋ 2 ERRORS ❋

When **eraser** was in the ninth row, it felt quite sad. Ⓔ But the words in the very back row would give anything to be able to sit in the ninth row. Ⓕ The ninth row was near the front of the bank. In fact, it was so close to the front of the bank that **run** couldn't even see it. Ⓖ

Anyhow, words got moved around every Friday, and the words that moved up cheered and shouted. The words that got moved toward

the back didn't act the same way. **(H)** Before the
big change took place, the word that got moved
the most rows was **summer. Summer** once

went from the fifteenth row to the seventh
row. **(I) Summer** didn't stay in the seventh row
very long. The move to the seventh row
happened during the summer when the weather
got very hot. People talked a lot about summer.
Then the weather cooled down, and **summer**
got moved back to the fifteenth row. **(J)**

As you know, words were always moved on Friday. But one Thursday, a big change took place, and the entire word bank was thrown into confusion.(K) Here's what happened. The people in Hohoboho began to do things.(L) The people began to swim and walk and eat and run. They began to look at things, kick things, and sit on things. They began to wonder, and sing, and dance.(M) The people talked about the things they did.(N) So the whooping and hollering in the word bank now came from a different part of the bank.(O) "Let's dance," the people would say, and a great cry went out from one of the rows.(P) "That's me," a word shouted.(Q)

"Dancing is fun," another person would say, and one of the relatives of **dance** would jump up. "That's me. People are talking about me."(R)

Things were crazy in the word bank. The words in the front of the bank turned around and looked and listened. They couldn't believe what was happening. There was still some shouting and yelling from the front of the word bank, but there was much more noise from the back of the bank. The words in the back were so happy that they were jumping and howling and bounding all over the place.

"Twenty times," the word **hop** said. "They said my name twenty times and the day isn't even over yet." Ⓢ

"That's nothing," **run** said, "I'm already up to 56." Ⓣ

Two words in the front row, **we** and **us,** were talking. **We** said, "Tomorrow is Friday. What do you think will happen to those words in the back row?"

"I don't know," **us** said. "We'll have to wait and see." Ⓤ 11 ERRORS

LESSON 63

1	2	3	4
island	notice	happier	squeezed
billow	announce	lifeboats	freeze
complete	forever	silent	fresh
except	noticed	beginner	easier
	announced	stumbled	beginning

5	6	7
salt	outline	**Vocabulary words**
thirstier	swept	**1.** neighbors
belly	tumbled	**2.** occasionally
salty	amazing	**3.** effort
bellies		**4.** currents
		5. announcement

B

LIFEBOATS

The story in the next lesson tells about lifeboats.Ⓐ A lifeboat is a small boat that is carried on a large ship like an ocean liner.Ⓑ People get in the lifeboats if the big ship starts to sink.Ⓒ

C

Run Gets MovedⒶ

It was the day that the words in the word bank got moved.Ⓑ

Here's how the words got moved every week. A voice would make the announcements about which words were to move. For example, the voice would say, "**Telephone** moves to row six." How would the voice announce that **me** has to sit in row three?Ⓒ

If a word was named in an announcement, the word would have to go to a new seat. The word would have to keep that seat until the voice announced that the word was to move again.Ⓓ ❋ 2 ERRORS ❋

The announcements in the word bank were made at 9:00 in the morning on Fridays. The announcements were usually over by 9:30.Ⓔ But on the Friday after the big change, all the words knew that things would be different.Ⓕ The words like **me** and **are** were interested in what would happen to those words in the back row. **Me** and **are** were so interested that they did not do much yelling and shouting when the people in Hohoboho said their names.Ⓖ

The words in the back row had been so happy that they were tired of yelling and shouting and feeling good.Ⓗ **Run** said to **walk,** "I don't really care if they move me or not. I feel great."

"Me too," the other word said.Ⓘ

At 9:00 the announcements began, and they were not finished until late at night.Ⓙ Nearly every word in the word bank was moved. Sometimes whole rows of words were moved. And some words moved more than 100 rows.Ⓚ The most amazing announcement of the day came about 10:30 in the morning after two or three hundred words had been moved. Here was that announcement: "The words **run** and **walk** will move from row 110 to row 1."Ⓛ

For a moment the word bank was silent. Some words turned to their neighbors and said, "Did that announcement say that **run** and **walk** will move to row 1?"

Run looked over at **walk.** They just stared at each other.Ⓜ Then they stood up and started to walk to the front row. Suddenly the words in the back row began to clap for them. Then they began to cheer.

"That's my relative," the word **walking** said. "That word used to sit right next to me."

There are only so many seats in each row. Two new words were moved to row one.Ⓝ So you know what had to happen to two words that were already in row one.Ⓞ The word **were** and the word **only** moved to row two. They were very mad.

Run sat in the seat that **were** had used. **Run** was next to some relatives of **were** who were still in the first row. One word was **are**.Ⓟ **Are** turned to **run** and said, "They'll probably move you back next week."

Run laughed and said, "I don't care. I'll remember this forever. This is great."

By the end of that Friday, **run** could turn around and talk to some of its relatives that were in row two.Ⓠ There were **running** and **ran. Runner** was in row five, but **runner** was very happy. "I never thought I would even see this part of the word bank," **runner** said.Ⓡ

When the next Friday came around, the words like **run** and **walk** and **jump** and the others kept their seats near the front of the word bank. In fact, they're still there. And **run** is no longer sad. In fact, **run** is happy all day and all night. **Run** yells and shouts and says, "That's me. I'm number one." And the other words that had been in the last row are happier than they ever thought they would be.Ⓢ ✸ 12 ERRORS ✸

LESSON 64

A

1	2	3
palm	noticed	billow
coconut	announced	except
myna	announcement	complete
	neighbors	completely
	island	billows

4	5	6
salty	outline	bubbles
beginner	sunk	patch
stumbled	brave	trail
swept	squeezed	bellies
tumbled		

7
Vocabulary words
1. notice
2. crate
3. currents
4. effort
5. occasionally

B

Linda and Kathy Escape from the Sinking Ship Ⓐ

"Fire! Fire!" a voice said over the loud-speaker. "The forward deck is on fire," the voice announced. "Everybody, leave the ship. Get into the lifeboats!" Ⓑ

Linda and her sister were on their way from the United States to Japan. Linda was thirteen years old, three years older than Kathy. Ⓒ Their father was in Japan, and they were on their way to visit him. Three days before, they had

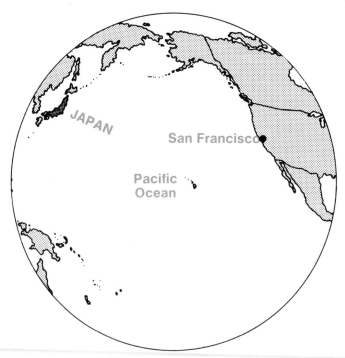

left California on a great ship called an ocean liner. They were now somewhere in the middle of the Pacific Ocean. Ⓓ

"Fire! Fire!" the voice shouted. "Everybody get into the lifeboats!" ❋ 2 ERRORS ❋

People were running this way and that way on the deck of the ship. They were yelling and crying. Ⓔ

"Hold on to my hand," Linda said. Ⓕ The girls went to the lifeboats. People were all around them, shoving and yelling. Linda could not see much. She was afraid. Ⓖ Suddenly she was no longer holding Kathy's hand. Ⓗ

Suddenly a strong pair of arms grabbed Linda. "In you go," a voice said. Ⓘ A big man picked Linda up and put her in the lifeboat.

"Where's my sister?" Linda asked. Linda looked but she couldn't see her younger sister. Ⓙ

"Kathy!" Linda called. Linda jumped from the lifeboat to the deck and started to look for her sister.

"Kathy! Kathy!" she called. There was so much noise on the deck that Linda could hardly hear her own voice.

Then she saw Kathy, who was standing behind a crowd of people. Kathy was crying. Ⓚ Linda ran over to her. "Hold my hand and don't let go," Linda said. Ⓛ

Linda noticed that the deck of the ship was leaning more and more. The ship was sinking.

She squeezed Kathy's hand and ran to the rail. Ⓜ "We've got to get into a lifeboat," Linda said out loud. She rubbed her eyes and tried to look for a lifeboat, but the front of the ship was hidden in smoke—black, rolling clouds of smoke. Ⓝ

"Hello," Linda shouted, "here we are." But

the smoke seemed to swallow her voice, and the roar of the fire made it sound very thin. **(O)**

Linda and Kathy walked along the rail at the stern of the ship. They looked into the water and called. But they couldn't see much. Occasionally, the smoke would clear and they would see the water below. **(P)**

Suddenly, the girls almost stumbled over a large wooden crate that was on the deck. **(Q)** "We'll use this for our lifeboat," Linda said. She and Kathy pushed the crate over the side. The boat was leaning so steeply now that it didn't take much effort to push the crate into the water. The crate disappeared in the water. **(R)**

"Here we go," Linda said. **(S)** Together, the girls jumped into the water. It was very warm and it tasted salty. **(T)** Linda was a good swimmer, but Kathy was a beginner. **(U)**

Behind them were great rushing sounds of water as the huge ocean liner continued to sink. As the ship went down, water rushed toward the ship, pulling everything in its path down with the ship. **(V)** The currents of water were pulling Linda and Kathy. Where was that crate? **(W)** ❋ 11 ERRORS ❋

LESSON 65

1	2	3	4
fresh	coconut	taste	swirl
easier	myna	ankle	print
freeze	palm	tasted	footprint
thirstier	coconuts	ankles	swirled
trail	bellies	tumbled	footprints

5	6
island	swept
completely	brave
billows	sunk
outline	bubbles
except	patch

B

Facts about Ocean Water

Today's story tells about ocean water.Ⓐ
Here are some facts about ocean water:

- Ocean water tastes salty because it has salt in it.Ⓑ
- If you drink a lot of ocean water, you'll get thirstier.Ⓒ
- A bottle of ocean water weighs more than a

bottle of fresh water because the ocean water has salt in it.(D)

- It's easier to float in ocean water.(E)
- Ocean water must get colder than fresh water before it will freeze.(F)

Look at the jars in the picture below. Figure out which jars are filled with ocean water.(G)

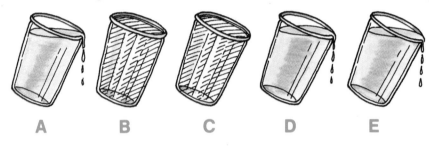

A   B   C   D   E

C

A Man and His Pets

A man had five fleas. When those fleas lined up end to end, they were _____ long.

The man had a pencil. It was a short pencil. So it weighed _____.

The man had three dogs. Two of them were the same size. They were a poodle and a pointer. They were _____ long. The third dog the man had looked something like a pointer, but it was shorter. It was brown and white and black. That dog could have been a

_____.

When the man went places without his car, he sometimes moved 20 miles per hour. Was he running or walking?

One of his dogs could run faster than he could. This dog could run 35 miles per hour. What kind of dog was it?

Sometimes the man would go in something that moved 5 hundred miles per hour. What did he go in?

These jets are so fast that they can fly from New York City to San Francisco in _____ hours. The flight from New York City to San Francisco is _____ miles.

D   *Liz Takes a Trip*

Liz liked cool weather. It was the middle of summer, and she wanted to go to a city that was cool in the summer. So she went to the city of _____.

Liz knew that the temperature of an object tells how _____ that object is. When she left New York City, the air on the ground was 30 degrees. But when the plane went higher and higher, the air outside the plane got _____.

When the plane was 6 miles high, the air outside the plane was below zero. It was

_____.

When the plane went from New York City to San Francisco, it was going in which direction?

The plane was facing the wind, so the name of the wind was a _____.

Did the plane go faster or slower than a plane going in the opposite direction?

The air that rushed from the jet engines was going to the east, so the jet engines moved toward the _____. The jet engines were attached to parts of the plane. Those parts were the _____.

As Liz flew along, she wanted to get a good look at things on the ground below. So she looked through something that makes things look very big. She looked through

_____. She saw the city of Chicago. That city was between Denver and

_____.

In San Francisco, Liz saw a lot of animals at a zoo. She knew how tall each animal was.

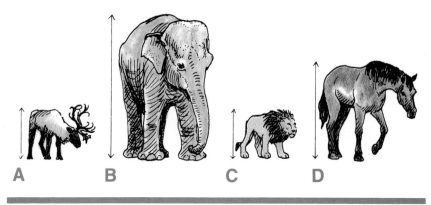

A   B   C   D

E

1	**2**	**3**
worst	continue	reach
outline	excitement	copilot
heaven	seventh	announcement
ninth	caught	effort
bulkhead	dodge	fifteenth
shove	compare	Thursday
captain	million	noticed
enemy	wonder	belong
forever	lifeboats	squeezed
degrees	warm-blooded	occasionally
world	neighbor	happier
fastened	search	current
distance	amazing	wander
corners	special	service
ocean	dead	easier

LESSON 66

1	2	3
juice	completely	patch
break	island	bubbles
echo	beginning	brave
liquid	except	sunk
circular	coconuts	wish-coooooo

4	5	6
swirled	fluffy	**Vocabulary words**
swept	bellies	**1.** billows
ankles	person	**2.** fade
footprints	beaks	**3.** outline
trail	tasted	**4.** tumbled

B

Facts about Islands

The story in the next lesson tells about an island. Ⓐ Here are facts about islands:

- Islands are small. Ⓑ
- There is water on all sides of an island. Ⓒ

There are three islands on the map below. Find them. Ⓓ

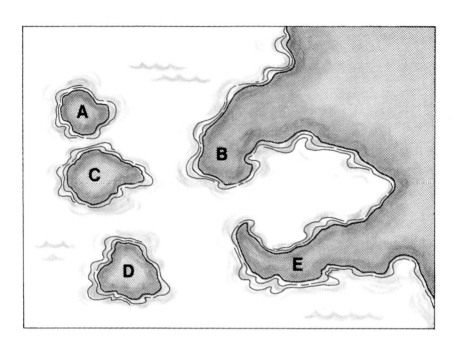

C

Linda and Kathy Find Land Ⓐ

The sinking ship was making great currents of water. These currents were pulling Linda and Kathy toward the ship. Only the prow of the ship was now above water. Ⓑ The prow was pointing into the air, and it was beginning to slip down into the water. The huge billows of smoke were beginning to clear. Ⓒ The currents were pulling harder and harder.Ⓓ

Linda and Kathy were swimming in the water. "There," Linda said, pointing to the crate. It was only a few meters from them.Ⓔ Linda swam as fast as she could. She swam and swam, but she couldn't seem to move in the current.Ⓕ ❋ 2 ERRORS ❋

At last she reached out and grabbed a corner of the crate. She climbed on. The crate was floating high in the water.Ⓖ Linda pulled Kathy onto the crate. "Let's paddle out of here before the current sucks us down with the ship," Linda said.Ⓗ So she and her sister got on their bellies and used their hands for paddles.Ⓘ They paddled as hard as they could. Behind them the rushing sounds began to fade.Ⓙ Linda turned around and saw just the tip of the prow sticking above the water. The rushing sounds faded completely, and the ocean became quiet.Ⓚ A huge trail of smoke still hung over the ocean, but there was no sign of the ship, except for a patch of water where bubbles were still coming up.Ⓛ Linda and Kathy looked and looked, but they could not see any of the lifeboats.

The girls sat on the crate with their feet in the water.Ⓜ The sun was hot. Linda tried to sleep, but the sun was too hot. Linda's feet were starting to burn. The salt water was making them very sore.

"I'm thirsty," Kathy said.Ⓝ

Linda said, "You can't drink the ocean water. It is full of salt. And salt water will just make you thirstier. You'll have to be brave. Someone will find us soon."

But noboby found them. They drifted farther and farther away from the place where the ocean liner had sunk. Slowly the sun went down.Ⓞ The air became cooler. Linda put her arm around Kathy and tried to sleep. She tried and tried, but she was too thirsty and her feet hurt too much.Ⓟ

Then she heard something in the dark: "Wish-coooooo, wish-cooooo, wish-cooooo."Ⓠ

"Those are waves," Linda said. "Those are waves on a beach. We must be near land. Kathy, we're near land."Ⓡ The girls looked in the direction of the sound. Linda could see the outline of trees.Ⓢ Yes, they were near a shore.Ⓣ

A wave crashed over their crate. The wave swept the crate faster and faster toward the shore. Linda had a nose full of water. She grabbed her sister and held on as hard as she could. The girls tumbled from the crate. Ⓤ They were in the water, but the water was not deep. In fact, they were sitting in water that was only a few centimeters deep.

They waded from the water and walked along the beach. It was so dark that they could hardly see where they were going.

"I'm thirsty," Kathy said. She sounded as if she was ready to cry.

"So am I," Linda said. "But it won't do us any good to cry." ❀ 11 ERRORS ❀

LESSON 67

A

1	2	3	4
footprints	coconuts	beaks	monkey
outcome	palm	echo	covered
raindrops	myna	break	person
become	liquid	juice	tasted
	fluffy	echoed	monkeys

5	6	7
explain	outer	**Vocabulary words**
raise	cracked	1. swirled
ankles	inner	2. foul
explained	leaked	
raised	circular	

B
FACTS ABOUT PALM TREES

Today's story tells about palm trees. Ⓐ Here are facts about palm trees:

- Palm trees grow in places that are very warm.**(B)**
- Palm trees cannot live in places that get cold.**(C)**
- Palm trees have very small roots.**(D)**
- The branches of palm trees are called fronds.**(E)**
- Some palm trees grow dates. Some palm trees grow coconuts.**(F)**

The picture shows a coconut palm tree. The parts are labeled.**(G)**

FRONDS

COCONUTS

TRUNK

ROOTS

C

Alone on an Island Ⓐ

Linda and Kathy walked along the beach. It was very dark, so they walked close to the waves. Ⓑ The waves washed up and swirled water around the girls' ankles. Ⓒ Then the waves fell back, pulling sand from under the girls' feet. Ⓓ Suddenly, Linda stepped into some very cold water, much colder than the water in the ocean. Ⓔ The water was running **into** the ocean. The girls were standing in a stream. Linda bent down and tasted the water. Ⓕ It was fresh water. "Kathy! Water!" she announced. Ⓖ

Kathy and Linda drank water until they couldn't drink any more. 🏵 2 ERRORS 🏵

Then they went to sleep. Linda didn't know how long she slept. A strange sound woke her up in the morning: "Caw chee, caw chee." Ⓗ There were many large birds around the girls and many trees. Some trees were palm trees, with trunks that have shelves like a ladder. Ⓘ The birds were different colors—some white, some red and yellow. Small black birds with yellow beaks made most of the noise. "I think those are myna birds," Linda said. "They're very smart."

"I'm hungry," Kathy said.

Linda stood up and looked around. She could see a beach of bright sand. She could see a blue sky and fluffy white clouds. She could see the ocean, stretching out until it met the sky. And she could see the crate, about twenty meters from the water. But she could not see a house, a boat, or any person other than her sister. Ⓙ

Linda said, "Let's walk down the beach and see if we can find out where we are."

"My feet hurt," Kathy said. Ⓚ

"We'll walk slowly," Linda said. So the girls started walking along the beach. They didn't go into the trees beyond the beach, because they were afraid that they would get lost. They walked and walked. They walked until the sun was high in the sky.Ⓛ But they did not see a house or a boat or any people.

They walked and walked until they came to a large rock. Linda climbed up on the rock and looked around. She saw footprints on the beach in front of her.Ⓜ The girls ran over to the footprints. Kathy said, ''Other people are here. I see their footprints.''

Linda looked at the footprints. There was a crate near the footprints. Linda said, "Those are **our** footprints. We have been walking in a circle. That means we are on an island. We walked all the way around the island."

Kathy started to cry.

Linda said, "Don't cry. Everything will be all right."

Linda didn't cry, but she felt like crying, too. She and her sister were all alone on an island. There was nothing on that island but trees and sand and a stream. How would they find food? How would they let anybody know where they were? How would they ever get off the island?Ⓝ ❋ 10 ERRORS ❋

LESSON 68

A

1	2	3	4
difficult	juice	inner	covered
exhausted	echoed	cracked	raindrops
strength	liquid	outer	circular
plunge	break	raised	hollered
fought	leaked	explained	

5	6	7
wheel	knives	noon
silver	edge	afternoon
become	ledge	head
monkeys	evening	overhead

8
Vocabulary words
1. outcome
2. echo
3. haul
4. ledge
5. foul

B

Facts about Coconuts

Here are facts about coconuts:Ⓐ

- A coconut is about as big as a football.Ⓑ
- Coconuts are not easy to open.Ⓒ
- Coconuts have two shells, one inside the other.Ⓓ
- Each shell is so hard that it wouldn't break if you hit it one time with a hammer.Ⓔ
- Inside the second shell is sweet, white coconut meat.Ⓕ
- Inside the coconut meat is sweet juice, called coconut milk.Ⓖ

The picture shows a coconut that is cut in half. The parts of the coconut are labeled.Ⓗ

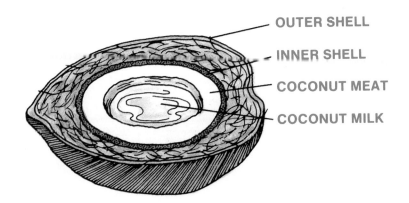

OUTER SHELL

INNER SHELL

COCONUT MEAT

COCONUT MILK

Linda and Kathy Find Some Food Ⓐ

Linda and Kathy were all alone on an island. Linda said, "Stop crying, Kathy. We are both very smart, and if we use our heads, we will get out of here." Ⓑ

Linda looked around and started to think. Then she pointed to the trees near the beach. "Those are **coconut** palm trees," she said to her sister. "Coconuts are good to eat. You can see them where the fronds join the trunk of the tree." Linda pointed. Ⓒ

The girls ran to the trees and started looking under them. Monkeys screeched at the girls from the trees.Ⓓ ❀ 2 ERRORS ❀

There were some coconuts on the ground, but they smelled foul and were covered with bugs.Ⓔ These coconuts were rotten. The girls kept looking. At last they found two good coconuts.Ⓕ

Kathy picked up one of the good coconuts and shook it. It sounded like a bottle that had water in it.Ⓖ Kathy said, "I'll break it open."Ⓗ She threw it down on the sand as hard as she could.Ⓘ The coconut made a dent in the sand, but there was no mark on the coconut.

Kathy picked up the coconut and slammed it down in the sand again. But the outcome was the same.Ⓙ

"I don't know how to do this," Kathy said.

"I've got an idea," Linda said, and she explained her idea to Kathy.Ⓚ

The girls walked along the beach until they came to the large rock. It was almost two meters across.Ⓛ Linda climbed up on the rock and held the coconut in both hands. She raised her hands over her head, and she threw the coconut

against the rock as hard as she could.Ⓜ
Kwack—the sound of the coconut echoed. But
there was no crack in the outer shell. Again
Linda held the coconut over her head, and
again the sound *kwack* echoed along the
beach.Ⓝ After two more tries, the outer shell
cracked open.Ⓞ

"Let me do it now," Kathy said, reaching
for the inner shell. Kathy slammed it against the
rock four times before it cracked. Linda grabbed
the cracked inner shell and held it so that not
much juice leaked out.Ⓟ Then Linda carefully
removed part of the shell. The girls ate all the
coconut meat and shared the coconut milk.Ⓠ

"I'm still hungry," Linda said. "What
about you?"

"Yes, me, too."

Linda said, "The trees are full of coconuts.
We have to think of some way of getting them."

The trees were very tall. "We can't climb up
there," Kathy said. "The coconuts are too
high."

Linda sat down and started to think. Then
she said, "I have an idea. I think I know how to
get the monkeys to help us."

The girls walked along the beach until they came to a place where there were many monkeys in the trees. The monkeys were making a lot of noise. They were jumping and running through the trees.

"Let's make them mad," Linda said.Ⓡ Linda walked over to the trees. The mother monkeys picked up their babies and screeched at Linda. "Choo, choo, cha, cha, chee, chee, chee," they screeched.Ⓢ

Linda made a face and waved her arms at them. The monkeys got madder and madder. Linda went over to one of the trees and tried to shake it.Ⓣ

One of the monkeys picked a coconut and threw it down at Linda. Linda tried to shake the tree again. Another monkey threw a coconut at her. Other monkeys started to throw coconuts. Coconuts were coming down like raindrops.Ⓤ

Linda ran away from the trees. By now the ground was covered with fresh coconuts.

Kathy laughed. "We will have enough coconuts to last us for days and days," she said.

 12 ERRORS

LESSON 69

A

1
gasoline
container
shallow
support
pour
liter

2
uphill
upstream
streambed
waterfall
afternoon
overhead

3
fought
plunged
strength
exhausted

4
clock
circular
knives
silver
clocks

5
constructed
solve
constructing
wheel

6
straight
straighten
struggle
angry
angrily

7
screech
reason
startled
flows

8
noon
steeper
difficult
evening

9
Vocabulary words
1. vines
2. haul
3. ledge

Facts about a Water Wheel

The story in the next lesson will tell about a water wheel. Ⓐ Here are some facts about a water wheel.

- A water wheel has a shaft. Ⓑ The shaft is labeled **1** in the picture. Ⓒ
- A water wheel has blades. Ⓓ One of the blades is labeled **2** in the picture. Ⓔ
- When water falls on a blade, the blade moves down. Ⓕ
- When the blade moves down, the shaft turns. Ⓖ The arrow in the picture shows which way the water is falling.

C

Making Tools Ⓐ

The only thing Linda and Kathy ate for two days was coconut meat. Ⓑ On the third day Kathy said, "I'm tired of eating coconuts. I want to eat something else."

"Me, too," Linda said. "I think that we should catch some fish." Ⓒ

Kathy said, "How can we catch fish without any fishing poles or hooks?"

Linda said, "We can take the wooden crate apart and use the nails for hooks. We can take vines from the jungle and use them for lines." Ⓓ

So the girls took the wooden crate apart. They pulled the nails out and bent them by hitting them with rocks. ❀ 2 ERRORS ❀

Then the girls found thin vines. They tied the vines to the nails. Linda said, "Now we need to put worms or bugs on our hooks."

They caught some big bugs and stuck them on the bent nails.Ⓔ

*Linda and her sister walked to a rocky place on the beach. They put their lines in the water and waited. They waited and waited. They could see many fish in the water—big fish, little fish. Some fish were green with red marks around their heads. Some fish were long and silver, like knives cutting through the water. Once in a while, a dark form of a large fish would move through the light green water.Ⓕ

The girls could see the fish, but the fish did not go after the bugs on the hook. The girls fished for two* hours. Finally, Kathy caught a fish, but it was only about ten centimeters long.Ⓖ

Kathy said, "We will never catch enough fish to have a fish dinner."

Linda said, "We have to think of another way to catch fish. Let's think."

The girls sat there on the sunny rocks and thought and thought. Finally Linda said, "I've got an idea. We will use a net. We will put the net in the water. When fish swim into the net, we will pull the net out of the water." **H**

The girls went back into the jungle and got lots of vines. Then they tied the vines together. Soon they had a net. It was very heavy. Kathy and Linda could hardly haul it along the beach.

They finally hauled the net to a ledge of rocks over the water. **I**

The girls dropped the net into the water and waited for fish to swim into the net. Soon, there were many fish inside the net. Some of them looked nearly as big as Kathy.Ⓙ

"Let's pull the net up," Linda said. "Pull fast."

The girls tried to pull the net out of the water. But the fish were pulling the net in the opposite direction.Ⓚ The fish pulled the net farther into the water. "We're slipping!" Kathy cried. Splash!Ⓛ Both of the girls fell into the water.

As the girls climbed back onto the rocks, Linda said, "We'll have to think of a better way to pull the net out of the water." ❄ 10 ERRORS ❄

LESSON 70

A

1	2	3	4
noon	afternoon	fought	solve
liter	support	exhausted	straighten
pounds	container	plunged	uphill
clocks	pour	difficult	struggle
gasoline	shallow	strength	upstream

5	6	7
angrily	streambed	**Vocabulary words**
reason	flows	1. evening
screech	steeper	2. overhead
become	constructing	3. constructed
pounds		4. startled

B

POUNDS

We use pounds to tell **how heavy things are.** Ⓐ The heavier something is, the more pounds it weighs. A five-pound brick weighs more than a four-pound brick. Ⓑ

Which weighs more, a man who weighs 150 pounds or a man who weighs 180 pounds? **C**

Here are some facts about pounds:

- A full-grown elephant weighs about 11 thousand pounds. **D**
- The book you are holding weighs a little more than one pound. **E**

How much do you weigh? **F**

C

Figuring Out the Time of Day

Linda and Kathy do not have any clocks, so they cannot tell exactly what time it is. But they can figure out if it is morning, noon, afternoon, evening, or night. To figure out the time, they use facts about the sun. **A**

Here are those facts:

- The sun always comes up in the east. **B**
- The sun always goes down in the west. **C**
- When the sun is right overhead, it is noon. **D**
- When the sun is coming up in the east, it is morning. **E**

- When the sun is going down in the west, it is afternoon.(F) ❋ 2 ERRORS ❋
- When the sun sets in the west, it is evening.(G)
- You know what time it is when it is dark.(H)

The picture below shows the sun at different times of day.(I)

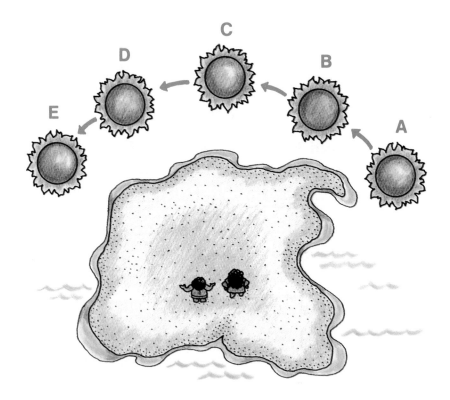

Touch sun A.(J) That is the first sun Linda and Kathy see in the morning. It is in the east.(K)

Touch sun B.Ⓛ That sun is moving up in the east. It is the sun they see later in the morning.

Touch sun C.Ⓜ This sun is right overhead. When they see this sun, they know what time of day it is.Ⓝ

Touch sun D.Ⓞ That sun is moving down in the west. It is an afternoon sun.Ⓟ

Sun E is the last sun they see. They know which direction it is.Ⓠ

Touch the sun that you see early in the morning.Ⓡ

In which direction is that sun?Ⓢ

Touch the last sun that you see at the end of the day.Ⓣ In which direction is that sun?Ⓤ

Touch the sun that you would see at noon.Ⓥ

If you know where the sun is, you can figure out directions. If you face the sun that you see early in the morning, in which direction are you facing?Ⓦ

If you face the sun that you see at the end of the day, in which direction are you facing?Ⓧ

❀ 6 ERRORS ❀